BULBS

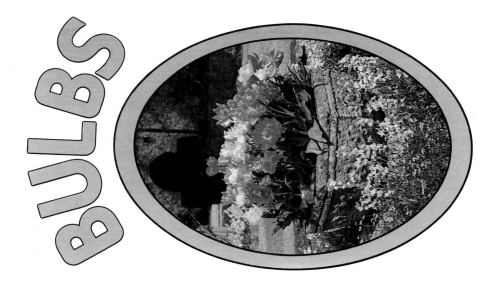

BULBS
H. G. Witham Fogg

Sundial

Contents

First published in 1980 by
Sundial Publications Limited
59 Grosvenor Street London W1

ISBN 0 906320 15 1
Printed in England by Severn Valley Press Limited

CHAPTER 1

Selecting Bulbs

Bulbous plants – including corms, rhizomes and tubers – are both beautiful and easy to grow. Together, they form an interesting and varied section of the world of flowers. Although their make-up is similar, they represent a huge variety of colours, shapes and sizes. Moreover, by careful selection, siting and planting, bulbs will provide colour in the garden throughout the year.

Since the origins of bulbs are so diverse, it is not possible to generalize treatment, therefore individual cultural details are given under respective headings. One notable fact, however, is that all bulbs, corms and tubers are storage organs which allow the plants to remain alive and healthy during long periods of dormancy, when they are without food or moisture. This is why bulbous plants can be dried off without coming to harm.

In addition, newly-acquired mature bulbs will produce flowers the first season that they are planted, since, in many cases, the flower bud has already formed in the bulb by planting time. This means that it is not until the second season and subsequent years, that the display depends on the general growing conditions and the skill of the gardener.

plate'. A corm is quite different, being more or less round, solid and somewhat flat, but still has a basal plate; those of crocuses and gladioli are examples. These shrivel after flowering, new corms having formed during the growing season.

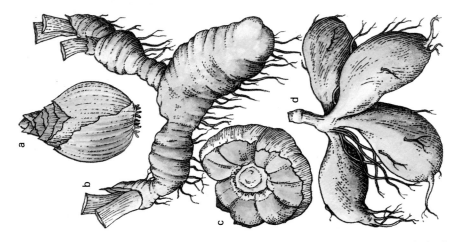

Left Anemone pavonina. *Long-lasting Peacock anemones are excellent for garden decoration and cutting.* **Below** *The different bulbous plants (a) a bulb (b) a rhizome (c) a corm showing root scar and (d) a tuber.*

Bulbs and their variations

There are structural differences between true bulbs and other bulbous plants and a brief mention should be made of these variations. A bulb, such as that of a daffodil, is a bud surrounded by fleshy or scaly leaves which rise from a flat disc or 'basal

Tubers are swollen underground stems. They vary in size and appearance but all are thick, short and solid, with eyes from which growth arises. They do not have scales or basal plates; examples are those of begonias, anemones and tropaeolums.

Rhizomes are similar to tubers. They may vary in thickness from a thread-like growth to the substantial size of those produced by flag irises. They usually grow horizontally. They prefer to be placed fairly near the surface, which often means that they spread freely: lily of the valley is an example of a free-spreading rhizome.

All of these structures have fibrous roots which are necessary for keeping the main portions in position as well as for obtaining essential nourishment and moisture. In addition, some corms, particularly gladioli and montbretias, produce two root systems. There is the fibrous system already mentioned and there is a thicker, sturdier system, known as contractile roots. These pull down the new corms which form on top of the old flowering corms and so keep them at the right depth.

All types, however, have the same life cycle due to their ability to store nutrients while dormant, which will be needed during the growing phase.

Apart from their colour variety and their adaptability many bulbs produce scents that rival the perfumes of modern cosmetic firms. Their foliage, too, is as attractive and diverse as the flowers themselves, while the blooms of most bulbs last well when cut which makes them ideal for use in flower arrangements.

Selecting bulbs

Good bulbs will be heavy for their size, with firm, plump flesh, free from bruises and scars, and their outer skins, except for tulips (which sometimes split or peel easily without harming the bulbs) will be intact. Dampness sometimes produces a grey film on the bulb, but this has no effect on its flowering ability: a gentle wipe with a soft cloth will remove the film.

Bulb sizes as indicated in catalogues are sometimes puzzling. Size is relevant only to bulbs and corms: tubers and rhizomes are not supplied by size.

In the case of hyacinths, the large 'exhibition size' is intended for showing and special purposes indoors, or for greenhouse cultivation. 'Top size' and, with the 'first size', is largely used for growing in pots indoors. 'Second size' hyacinths are next in quality to 'first size', followed by 'bedding hyacinths', both of which are more suitable for outdoor planting.

Narcissi or daffodils are often offered as 'mother' bulbs. This is the largest size, the next trade sizes being 'double' and then 'single-nosed'.

Tulips and gladioli sizes are in centimetres, measured at the largest circumference point. Weight, rather than size, however, is often a better guide to quality.

Gladioli corms vary considerably in size. Size is governed by the conditions under which they have been grown as well as by their age. A good guide is the circular root scar at the base: whatever the size of the corm, a small root scar indicates youth. Jumbo corms are sometimes offered but it is better to plant smaller, heavier corms.

It pays to order bulbs early, not only because one can then usually be

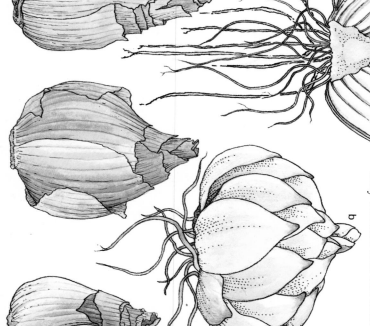

(a) A cross section of a bulb showing the growing flower (b) The imbricated scales of a lilium bulb (c) The various sizes of a narcissus bulb as described in catalogues. Shown, from left to right, are a 'mother' bulb, a 'double-nosed' bulb, a 'single-nosed' bulb and finally an offset. Right Mixed hyacinths are invaluable for colour and fragrance.

sure of getting exactly what is wanted, but because most bulbs grow better if they are not kept out of the ground too long. In the case of liliums, where the bulb scales are thick and overlapping (often described as 'imbricated'), they should not be left dry or uncovered, for they will become limp and flabby and will take a long time to recover. Such bulbs are sometimes seen for sale outside shops or in market places; they should be ignored, even if they are cheap.

When bulbs are stored after lifting or are received from the supplier before they can be planted, they should be placed in a dry, well-aired place. They should never be kept in closely fastened bags or boxes or they will become soft. When they are left in bags for a few days, the tops of the bags should be opened and a few air holes made.

The three planting seasons

Provided the soil is well-drained, there are species and varieties of bulbs that will grow anywhere in any garden, in sun, shade or semi-shade; in grass; in rock gardens and shrubberies; and in woodland areas. Out of the full sun the flowers last longer. To obtain bulb flowers all the year round it is necessary to plan three planting seasons.

Bulbs planted in autumn, including daffodils, hyacinths and tulips, will, according to the species used, flower from January to June in the garden. These are usually referred to as spring-flowering.

Summer-flowering bulbs, such as acidantheras, gladioli and sparaxis, can be planted from March to May. Those that flower in autumn should be planted from early August onwards. These include *Crocus longi-*

florus, C. sativus, C. speciosus, C. zonatus, Crinum powellii, Nerine bowdenii, Sternbergia lutea, Cyclamen europaeum, C. neapolitanum and *Zephyranthes candida.*

Bulbs do not ask much of the gardener. The regular removal of weeds (except in naturalized areas) so that the plants can grow properly and obtain the benefit of rains, and the picking off of faded flowers, are all that is usually needed. There should, of course, be the occasional inspection so that any pests or disorders can be detected and dealt with in their earliest stages.

Occasionally tulips fail to flower or grow properly. This is often due to planting in hard, packed-down soil preventing the root caps from softening and thus imprisoning the roots beneath. Excepting in the case of offsets or small divisions, or where long established clumps of bulbs

OUTDOOR BULB-PLANTING CHART

BULB	DEPTH TO PLANT	SUN OR ‡SHADE	§DISTANCE APART
*Acidanthera	7.5cm (3in)	Sun	15cm (6in)
Allium	5–8cm (2–3in)	Sun	10–15cm (4–6in)
Alstroemeria	13–15cm (5–6in)	Sun	13–15cm (5–6in)
Amaryllis belladonna	15–20cm (6–8in)	Sun/Shade	30cm (1ft)
Anemone	5cm (2in)	Sun/Partial shade	10–15cm (4–6in)
*Babiana	7.5cm (3in)	Sun	13–15cm (5–6in)
Brodiaea	10cm (4in)	Sun	10cm (4in)
Camassia	7.5cm (3in)	Sun/Partial shade	38–45cm (15–18in)
Cardiocrinum giganteum	3–5cm (1–2in)	Sun/Partial shade	30–60cm (1–2ft)
Chionodoxa	7.5cm (3in)	Sun/Semi-shade	10cm (4in)
Colchicum	7.5cm (3in)	Sun/Semi-shade	7.5cm (3in)
Crinum	15cm (6in)	Sun	30cm (1ft)
*Crocosmia	8–10cm (3–4in)	Sun/Semi-shade	13–15cm (5–6in)
Crocus	10cm (4in)	Sun/Semi-shade	7.5–10cm (3–4in)
Cyclamen	4cm (1½in)	Sun/Semi-shade	15cm (6in)
*Dahlia	15cm (6in)	Sun	45–90cm (18in–3ft)
Endymion	8cm (3½in)	Semi-shade	10–15cm (4–6in)
Eranthis	4cm (1½in)	Sun/Semi-shade	5cm (2in)
Erythronium	10–15cm (4–6in)	Semi-shade	10cm (4in)
*Freesia	7.5cm (3in)	Semi-shade	7.5cm (3in)
Fritillaria meleagris	7.5–10cm (3–4in)	Sun/Semi-shade	15cm (6in)
Galanthus	13cm (5in)	Sun	13cm (5in)
Galtonia	10–13cm (4–5in)	Sun/Partial shade	15–17cm (6–7in)
*Gladiolus	7.5cm (3in)	Sun	15cm (6in)
Hermodactylus	10–15cm (4–6in)	Sun	13cm (5in)
Hyacinth	7–8cm (3–4in)	Sun/Semi-shade	10–13cm (4–5in)
Iris (Dutch)	7–8cm (3–4in)	Sun/Semi-shade	7.5cm (3in)
*Ixia	7.5cm (3in)	Sun	7.5–10cm (3–4in)
Ixiolirion	8–10cm (3–4in)	Sun/Partial shade	10–15cm (4–6in)
Leucojum	10cm (4in)	Sun/Partial shade	30–60cm (1–2ft)
Lilium (bulb-rooting)	7.5cm (3in)	Sun/Partial shade	7.5cm (3in)
Lilium (stem-rooting)	15–20cm (6–8in)	Sun/Partial shade	7–10cm (3–4in)
Muscari	5–8cm (2–3in)	Sun/Semi-shade	5–8cm (2–3in)
Narcissus	8–13cm (3–5in)	Sun/Partial shade	13cm (5in)
*Nerine	5–8cm (2–3in)	Sun/Partial shade	30cm (1ft)
Ornithogalum	7.5cm (3in)	Sun	7.5cm (3in)
Puschkinia	7.5cm (3in)	Sun/Partial shade	7.5cm (3in)
Ranunculus	5cm (2in)	Sun/Semi-shade	7–10cm (3–4in)
Scilla	7.5cm (3in)	Sun/Semi-shade	7.5cm (3in)
*Sparaxis	5cm (2in)	Sun/Shade	10cm (4in)
Sternbergia	11–13cm (4–5in)	Sun	7.5cm (3in)
*Tigridia	5–8cm (2–3in)	Sun	15–20cm (6–8in)
Tulip	11–13cm (4–5in)	Sun/Semi-shade	13–15cm (5–6in)
*Zantedeschia	11–13cm (4–5in)	Sun/Semi-shade	60cm (2ft)

* indicates bulbs which should be lifted in autumn
§ applies to planting in lines or groups
‡ semi-shade is varying light as the sun moves round; partial shade is permanent

Details for Bulbocodium are the same as for Crocus
Details for Merendera are the same as for Colchicum
Details for Montbretia are the same as for Crocosmia

Details for Ipheion are the same as for Brodiaea
Details for Triteleia are the same as for Brodiaea
Details for Lapeirousa cruenta are the same as for Ixia
Details for Anomatheca cruenta are the same as for Ixia

have divided and need to rest from flowering, lift the bulbs when the foliage has faded and replant immediately in looser soil.

Scent

The dramatic and exciting colour range of bulbs, combined with their attractive shapes, tend to hide the fact that many are delightfully scented. The sweet fragrance of the hyacinth, especially when grown in bowls in the living room, is well known, but there is a surprising range of bulbs that emit scents of varying strength and sweetness. The following is a short alphabetical list; all are fully described, together with many other perfumed species, in Chapter Four.

Allium neapolitanum, Crocus biflorus, Gladiolus tristis, Iris bakeriana, Iris reticulata, Leucojum vernum, Liliums in variety, *Muscari botryoides* and its white form, *Muscari plumosum.*

Narcissus in variety, including *N. campernelle, N. jonquilla, N. albus plenus odoratus, N. tazetta* and *N. poeticus; Brodiaea uniflora* and various tulip species.

There are a number of named tulip hybrids and varieties that are fragrant, including early singles, and Bellona, General de Wet, and Prince of Austria.

The late double tulip Eros is distinctly perfumed and some fragrance can be found in several of the Parrot varieties.

History

Many of the bulbous plants we know so well came originally from many different parts of the world, sometimes at great cost and even risk of life to travellers, merchants, plant hunters, soldiers or missionaries. By cultivation, selection and hybridization, some have been greatly improved in size, strength, colour, flowering ability and resistance to disorders and pests.

Anemone coronaria, the Poppy anemone, originated in corms being sent from Turkey to the Dutch botanist Clusius, towards the end of the sixteenth century. They were subsequently cultivated with success in both France and England. Their official name today is *Anemone de Caen.* The begonia is a wild plant in Mexico and in parts of South America. The botanist and monk, Plumier, is credited with the discovery of this plant in Mexico in 1690. He could not place it in any known genus and named it after Michael Begon, a French botanist who was the Governor of Santa Domingo. It was first seen in Britain in 1857 when it arrived at Kew Gardens. Since then many species have been found and much hybridization has been carried out.

The name crocus comes originally from a Greek word. Many species come from Greece and Asia Minor, while the large-flowered varieties were raised in Holland. *Crocus sativus,* the Saffron Crocus, is said to have been taken to a village in Essex (Walden) by a pilgrim about 1330 A.D. The prefix 'Saffron' was later applied to this village because of the flourishing of the saffron industry which became established there, several centuries afterwards. This has long since finished and Spain is now one of the modern sources of saffron.

The freesia has had several name changes. About one hundred years ago it was known as *Freesia refracta.* Later it was listed as a tritonia, then as an ixia. In 1866 it became a separate genus, named after Frederick Freese, a German doctor.

The gladiolus derives its name from the Latin 'gladius', a sword, referring to the shape of the leaves. There are many species, mostly natives of South Africa. Much hybridization has been carried out, notably in Britain, Holland, France and the United States. This has led to the production of the many named hybrids now in cultivation. *Gladiolus primulinus* was a notable find in the rain forests near the Victoria Falls on the Zambesi river in 1902. This dainty species has been much used in creating marvellous strains of elegant plants in a wide colour range.

Gloxinias originated in Brazil. Named after P. B. Gloxin of Strasburg, the first record of this plant appeared in 1785 but it was not until 1817 that the plant came to Britain. Botanists have decided that it belongs to the genus *Sinningia,* but, since its original name is so popular, few people use the correct title.

Hyacinthus, son of King Amyclas, was a young man of great beauty and attraction. He was loved by both Apollo and Zephyr. The latter, in her jealousy, threw a discus at Hyacinthus and killed him, whereupon Apollo is said to have made a flower grow where his blood was shed.

The iris flower has been portrayed in one form or another in paintings, pottery, embroidery and heraldic designs for countless years. Centuries ago it was adopted as the badge of the French royal family and Louis XII used it as his emblem, known as the *Fleur de Lys.*

The lily is another ancient flower, many species coming from China, Japan, Korea and Tibet; others are natives of Europe, Asia Minor and Palestine. There is great current interest in liliums, fostered by the Royal Horticultural Society which has a special group and year book devoted to the flower.

Narcissi have been in cultivation for centuries. The genus is named after the youth in the Greek legend who was changed into this flower. Much hybridization has taken place and the family is now divided into ten distinct groups, of which the large trumpet variety, known as daffodils, is one.

Tulips were unknown in Western Europe before the middle of the sixteenth century. The first general reference to the tulip is contained in a letter written by the ambassador of Ferdinand I, Emperor of Austria, at the court of the Sultan of Turkey. He wrote that everywhere he went he was offered an abundance of tulips, which the Turks called 'tulipan'.

Later came the Dutch 'tulip mania' and subsequent crash. The tulip mania began when rich people from Vienna and Dutch merchants bought bulbs from Turkey. In the mid-seventeenth century, tulip markets were established in Amsterdam, Haarlem, Leiden and Enkhuizen, where bulbs were bought and sold for enormous sums. After a time, the popularity of the bulb declined, the crash coming in 1636, when all holders tried to sell their bulbs but with little business being done. Today there are thousands of varieties in cultivation, varying considerably in height and size; there are many beautiful species, some with most attractive foliage.

CHAPTER 2

Planting and Growing Bulbs

Types of soil

There are, of course, many types of soil including loamy, peaty, chalky, limey or clay. Fortunately the majority of bulbs are very adaptable and will grow in most soils except those that remain wet and sticky. Sandy soil is apt to dry out quickly, while very chalky ground causes chlorosis or yellowing of the leaves, resulting in poor growth.

A good loamy soil is ideal for bulbs. All ground can be improved by working in plenty of humus and similar crumb-forming materials, such as leaf mould, peat, bark fibre and 'ripe' compost. Humus is the brown or black substance resulting from the slow decomposition of organic matter. It is advisable, wherever possible, to make and maintain a compost heap. Either dig in the humus whilst the soil is being moved or sprinkle it in the furrows or holes at planting time.

Manures and fertilizers

All soils contain reserves of the plant foods required by growing crops, but the addition of various organic manures when the ground is being prepared will be rewarded by more and better flowers. The aim should be to feed the soil, and not merely to feed the plants when they are in growth or looking unhealthy.

Disappointments sometimes occur when growing plants are fed with artificial or powder fertilizers; some

of these encourage quick growth which cannot stand up to normal climatic conditions. Plants grown in well-fed soil make a strong root system which not only produces robust top growth and plenty of flowers, but is less liable to attacks by pests and disorders.

Where it is intended that bulbs should remain in position for some years, it is advisable to move the soil fairly deeply, say 38 cm (15 in) or more and to work into the bottom of this depth a good layer of compost, peat, leaf mould or similar bulky material. The addition of a good sprinkling of bone meal into the top 15 to 23 cm (6 to 9 in) feeds the bulbs without encouraging quick, flimsy growth. Humus or organic matter darkens the soil and increases its power to absorb the sun's rays, so that it warms up more quickly in spring. It also provides plant foods such as nitrogen, phosphates and potash. On soil which is naturally very light and sandy, and thus quick to dry out, it is a good plan to mulch growing plants with leaf mould, peat or bark fibre. This should be done when the surface is moist but not, of course, when it is frost bound.

Aerating the soil

It is important that the soil in which bulbous plants (or, in fact, any other type of plant) are grown has adequate aeration with good drainage and contains plenty of bulky organic matter in order that the beneficial soil organisms can do their work and make the ground more productive. Earthworms also play an important

Narcissus Carlton. Suitable for garden decoration and forcing.

part in keeping the soil healthy. They breed and grow most freely when there are ample quantities of organic matter in the soil. Worms help to aerate the ground by drawing dead leaves and other material into their holes, and the tunnels they make allow water a free passage.

Planting

At whatever time of year it is intended to plant bulbs, beds and borders should be prepared well in advance so that the ground has time to settle. If this is not done, the soil around the planted bulbs may sink, and water may settle in the depressions, causing the bulbs to decay.

Depth of planting, i.e. the amount of soil covering the bulb, can have a great effect on development. Bulbs are often not planted deeply enough. A few need shallow burying, the most notable being ismene, *Lilium candidum* and *Cardiocrinum giganteum*, which need a covering of only 2.5 to 5cm (1 to 2in). Anemones and ranunculuses need not be buried more than 5cm (2in). It is not the size of the bulb or corm that determines the planting depth for, as is indicated in the table on page 15, gladiolus corms should be placed as deeply as the larger daffodil and tulip bulbs. If gladiolus is planted shallowly, the weight of the spikes causes the whole plant to topple over. Deeper planting is also needed in exposed or windy positions for the same reason.

There are several types of bulb planters available. The simplest is a trowel with a blade of normal width; another type having a long, narrow blade. The special bulb planters which have a long handle and step between them.

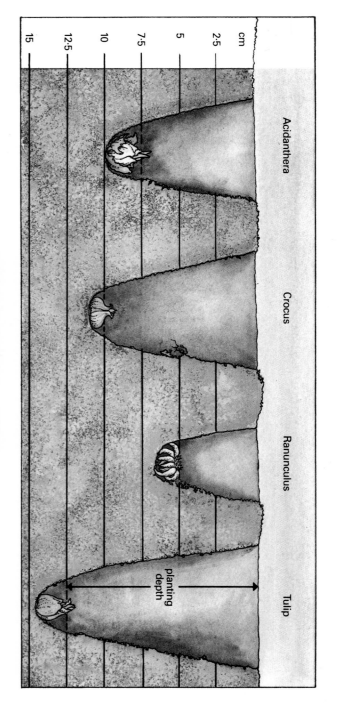

Above *Examples to show the correct planting depth.* **Left** *Using a bulb planter to take out a cup of soil.*

for pressing into the soil, take out a neat hole, even in turf, large enough for a good-sized bulb.

The time of planting is also important. Most spring-flowering bulbs can be planted during August, September and October although, when moving to a new garden, I have planted as late as early December and still obtained reasonably good results. An exception to this general rule is the tulip, of which the early single and double varieties, the Darwin, cottage and spring-flowering species, are best planted in October and November. If planted before this time, the tops of the young shoots are liable to frost damage and the subsequent discoloration persists throughout the season.

It is best to plant bulbs in groups or beds of one variety, particularly in the case of tulips, hyacinths and daffodils. Scattered in small numbers, they fail to provide their delightful splash of colour. Moreover, several different species or varieties in one bed or border are unlikely to flower at exactly the same time. Spacing depends upon the effect one wants to create, but all bulbs like breathing space. Ideally tulips, hyacinths and daffodils should be planted at least 13cm (5in) apart and most small bulbs need 7 to 10cm (3 to 4in) space between them.

cm
2·5
5
7·5
10
12·5
15

Acidanthera Crocus Ranunculus Tulip

planting depth

BULB CALENDAR

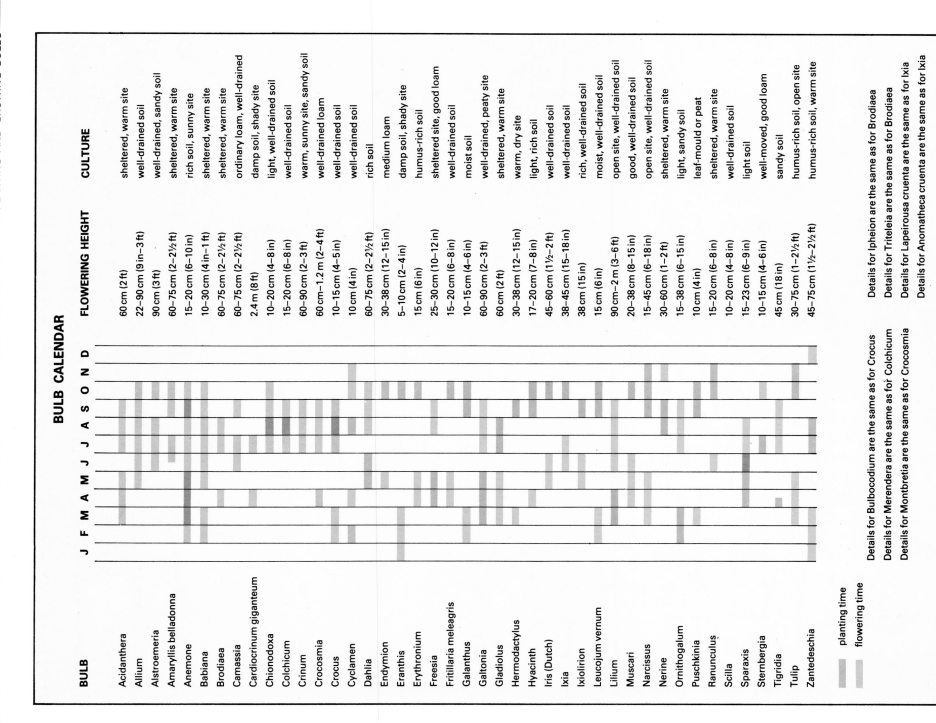

BULB	J F M A M J J A S O N D	FLOWERING HEIGHT	CULTURE
Acidanthera		60 cm (2 ft)	sheltered, warm site
Allium		22–90 cm (9 in–3 ft)	well-drained soil
Alstroemeria		90 cm (3 ft)	well-drained, sandy soil
Amaryllis belladonna		60–75 cm (2–2½ ft)	sheltered, warm site
Anemone		15–20 cm (6–10 in)	rich soil, sunny site
Babiana		10–30 cm (4 in–1 ft)	sheltered, warm site
Brodiaea		60–75 cm (2–2½ ft)	sheltered, warm site
Camassia		60–75 cm (2–2½ ft)	ordinary loam, well-drained
Cardiocrinum giganteum		2.4 m (8 ft)	damp soil, shady site
Chionodoxa		10–20 cm (4–8 in)	light, well-drained soil
Colchicum		15–20 cm (6–8 in)	well-drained soil
Crinum		60–90 cm (2–3 ft)	warm, sunny site, sandy soil
Crocosmia		60 cm–1.2 m (2–4 ft)	well-drained loam
Crocus		10–15 cm (4–5 in)	well-drained soil
Cyclamen		10 cm (4 in)	well-drained soil
Dahlia		60–75 cm (2–2½ ft)	rich soil
Endymion		30–38 cm (12–15 in)	medium loam
Eranthis		5–10 cm (2–4 in)	damp soil, shady site
Erythronium		15 cm (6 in)	humus-rich soil
Freesia		25–30 cm (10–12 in)	sheltered site, good loam
Fritillaria meleagris		15–20 cm (6–8 in)	well-drained soil
Galanthus		10–15 cm (4–6 in)	moist soil
Galtonia		60–90 cm (2–3 ft)	well-drained, peaty site
Gladiolus		60 cm (2 ft)	sheltered, warm site
Hermodactylus		30–38 cm (12–15 in)	warm, dry site
Hyacinth		17–20 cm (7–8 in)	light, rich soil
Iris (Dutch)		45–60 cm (1½–2 ft)	well-drained soil
Ixia		38–45 cm (15–18 in)	well-drained soil
Ixiolirion		38 cm (15 in)	rich, well-drained soil
Leucojum vernum		15 cm (6 in)	moist, well-drained soil
Lilium		90 cm–2 m (3–6 ft)	open site, well-drained soil
Muscari		20–38 cm (8–15 in)	good, well-drained soil
Narcissus		15–45 cm (6–18 in)	open site, well-drained soil
Nerine		30–60 cm (1–2 ft)	sheltered, warm site
Ornithogalum		15–38 cm (6–15 in)	light, sandy soil
Puschkinia		10 cm (4 in)	leaf-mould or peat
Ranunculus		15–20 cm (6–8 in)	sheltered, warm site
Scilla		10–20 cm (4–8 in)	well-drained soil
Sparaxis		15–23 cm (6–9 in)	light soil
Sternbergia		10–15 cm (4–6 in)	well-moved, good loam
Tigridia		45 cm (18 in)	sandy soil
Tulip		30–75 cm (1–2½ ft)	humus-rich soil, open site
Zantedeschia		45–75 cm (1½–2½ ft)	humus-rich soil, warm site

planting time

flowering time

Details for Bulbocodium are the same as for Crocus
Details for Merendera are the same as for Colchicum
Details for Montbretia are the same as for Crocosmia

Details for Ipheion are the same as for Brodiaea
Details for Triteleia are the same as for Brodiaea
Details for Lapeirousia cruenta are the same as for Ixia
Details for Anomatheca cruenta are the same as for Ixia

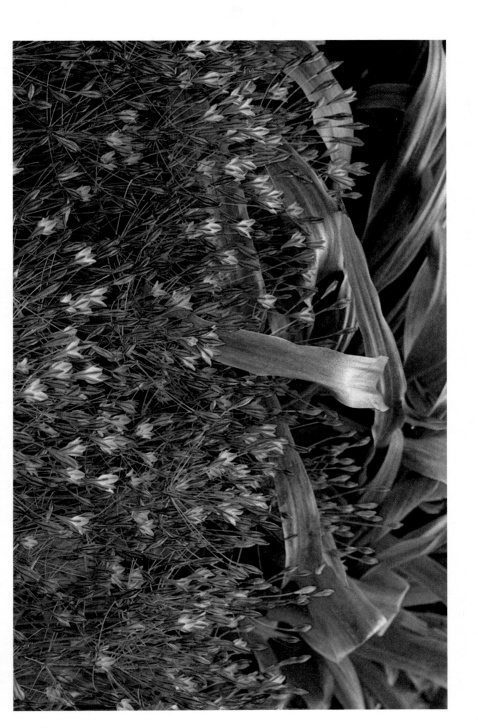

Growing

During the growing process, bulbs need the minimum of attention. They should, however, be kept free from weeds. When hoeing or otherwise pulling out weeds, make sure not to damage leaves or stems, nor to disturb the bulbs when removing nearby plants or weeds. Once the petals have faded it is best to remove the old flower head so that seeds do not form. If seeds are allowed to develop, this weakens the bulbs and affects any developing bulblets or cormlets. To obtain seeds from a particular flower, first mark and support the stems, then keep a close watch on them so that the seeds are not lost (see Chapter Eight).

The leaves of bulbous plants should be allowed to die down naturally since it is during this process that the bulbs are built up for the following year. It sometimes happens that it is necessary to remove daffodils, tulips, etc., before they have com-

Above *Free-flowering brodiaeas soon increase rapidly from self sown seeds.* **Below** *Cutting off gladioli stems after lifting corms.*

16

pleted their growth in order to make way for summer bedding plants. In such cases they should be lifted carefully and moved to another position, making sure that the bulbs are well covered so that the foliage dies down naturally. It is not necessary to water established bulbs. However, in an extremely dry season, one or two good soakings can be given, so that the foliage keeps a good colour until the flowers fade.

Few bulbs require staking, but some taller types such as lilies and gladioli will benefit from supports in gardens subjected to strong winds.

Lifting

Many bulbs can be left in position for some years, although it is wise to lift tulips annually. By so doing the risk

of 'tulip fire' (see Chapter Nine) is made far less likely. Tulip fire is often induced and will spread in damp weather. The spores settle on the foliage, then descend to the bulbs where they overwinter. When bulbs are lifted in summer, they can be checked and the risk is minimized.

Use a fork for lifting, not a spade. Mark, with a small stick or label, the location of bulbs planted in areas where soil movement is likely to be carried out after the bulbs have finished flowering and, therefore, show no top growth.

If bulbs are injured at any time, smooth the edges of the wounds and dust with yellow sulphur powder. On removal from the soil, all dead foliage should be taken off and the bulbs laid out to dry in an airy place. It is important to ensure that they are

completely dry before being stored, for even a little moisture between the scales can lead to mildew and decay.

The treatment of bulbous subjects lifted in autumn, such as the corms of gladiolus and montbretia, must necessarily be different where there is a heavy rainfall and a humid atmosphere. In these cases, the corms should be lifted once the foliage begins to turn yellow. Though the main stem may be cut off at lifting time (about 5 cm (2 in) above the new corm which forms above the old, now shrivelled corm), the plants can be left for a week or so in a dry, airy place before being stored in trays or shallow boxes; avoid a dry, warm atmosphere.

Small quantities can be kept in strong paper bags with air holes cut to allow ventilation.

Use a fork for lifting bulbous plants once their foliage has died down. Remove all dead foliage and any loose skins. Trim the roots and once the bulb is completely dry store in an airy place such as shallow boxes or paper bags with air holes.

CHAPTER 3

Colourful Beds and Borders

Preparation

Whatever the size or purpose of a bed or border in which bulbs are to be planted, the basic method of preparing the site is the same. Much, however, depends on the type of soil, what was grown there previously, and whether persistent perennial weeds are present. Many bulbs can be allowed to remain in position for two or three years or even longer. This makes it important to prepare the site well and to ensure that deep-rooted weeds, such as docks, thistles and ground elder, are removed, as well as any couch grass and convolvulus. Such pre-planting attention will save a lot of work later.

Except for a very few which like moist conditions, bulbs need good drainage. Dig deeply over the whole bed or border. This is better than making holes or separate patches where bulbs are to be planted, although this may sometimes have to be done where vacant spaces are being filled. The addition of decayed organic matter when the soil is being moved will improve all ground; it helps to ensure drainage where there is a heavy clay soil and holds sandy soil particles together.

Soil containing plenty of humus retains moisture and nutrients and encourages the beneficial soil organisms to do their work. Once bulbs are established, top dressing or mulching the beds with compost will encourage continuing growth. A layer of up to 5 cm (2 in) deep is ideal.

Before planting, try to visualize the effect when the bulbs are in full growth and flowering. This includes the surroundings – whether the site is sunny or shaded, open or wind-swept, and what other colourful subjects are likely to be in bloom when the bulbs flower.

Planting

Bulbs can be planted in groups or singly or combined with other flowering plants, including any spring and summer bedding arrangements.

Left *On a less grand scale, this attractive merging of colours and shapes can be achieved in private gardens.* **Right** *Scented Lilium regale for garden and pots.*

They can be clustered in appropriate spaces in borders containing perennial plants, shrubs and evergreens. They also look well in lawn beds or in borders near pools, terraces and retaining walls.

Many gardeners have been faced with the difficult choice of whether to leave particular blooms for show in the garden or to cut the flowers for home decoration. The obvious reason for planting bulbs is to provide a colourful display in beds and borders. One solution is to plant bulbs for cutting in a special bed, reserved for this purpose. Second- or third-year bulbs can also be moved to less prominent positions, where the blooms can be cut for indoor display. A small cutting bed can also be used as an experimental plot for new or expensive varieties, to give the gardener an idea of their quality and to act as a colour guide for positioning in beds the following season.

Suitable subjects for cutting include varieties of allium, anemone, brodiaea, camassia, hyacinth, iris, ixia, ixiolirion, narcissus, sparaxis and tulip, but one must not forget the smaller types of bulbs such as snowdrops, chionodoxas, grape hyacinths and scillas, which are rarely considered as cut flowers but which make delightful smaller arrangements. The smaller flowers can be gathered from general garden plantings without being missed, but are well worth the small space they take up in a cutting garden.

Spring bulbs for cutting can also be interplanted with other flowers which bloom later, and even with vegetables on a rotation system, so that maximum use is made of available space. After all, such bulbs are utilizing winter space in the garden and can easily be lifted when their foliage has faded to make room for the flowers and vegetables whose planting time follows their blooming.

Beds and borders become the focal points in any garden and whatever their shape – even where bulbs are planted in blocks of single colour or in patterned designs of various colours and shades – they look good when the groups vary in size and have irregular or curved outlines rather than a geometric form.

Beds and borders tend to be distinguished by whether they are formal or informal. A bed is replanted each time one set of bulbs has finished flowering. Bulbs in a border are left from year to year, although some borders are replanted seasonally with later-flowering subjects.

Where more than one kind are being planted, particularly in a small bed, care and taste must be exercized in selecting varieties that will not only provide the desired colour combinations but will also flower together in order to provide a reasonable display. Further thought must be given where other flowering subjects are being grown in the same bed or border. In the case of the spring-flowering hyacinths, daffodils and

Crocuses in a mixture of colours make a feature of an otherwise bare border.

tulips, useful subjects to grow in the same beds as a colourful ground cover include aubrieta, yellow alyssum, primroses, violas, polyanthuses and forget-me-nots, which together produce a long-lasting effect. Mixtures of bulbs such as crocuses, narcissi, hyacinths and tulips can also be used.

The height of the flowers is another important point to observe when planting (see the Bulb Calendar on page 10 for details). Obviously the taller growing bulbs should be sited near the back, the shorter towards the front. With a two-sided, or all round border, the taller varieties will be placed towards the centre.

Hardy ornithogalum and muscari, Heavenly Blue, make an imposing spring display.

The time of flowering should also be considered so that there is continuous colour and so that all the bulbs can be seen at their best. This will prevent such mistakes as planting tall, May-flowering tulips in front of the shorter-stemmed, single, early varieties, for these would be partly hidden at least by the leafy foliage of the later varieties.

In beds containing other plants, bulbs such as narcissus and allium, which are being left in position, should be planted behind later-flowering perennials which will grow and hide the yellowing foliage after the flowers have faded.

Colour patterns

As it is possible to grow a succession of different bulbous plants that will flower throughout the year, it is advisable to check the flowering dates of other plants, trees and shrubs in the garden, so that interesting colour pictures can be produced over a long period.

Varying garden levels provide opportunities for creating distinctive colour pictures. Hyacinths, for example, because of their sturdiness, look attractive at any height. Autumn-flowering cyclamen seen round the base of trees or shrubs, at either a higher or lower level than the sur-

rounding ground, always command attention and once established they soon increase in numbers. Apart from specially made beds and borders in the open garden, informal, mixed borders can be established along the base of house walls or be extended in sweeping curves along the drive or a wooded copse, alongside a stream or even on the banks of a drainage ditch. Informal borders can also be located against a garden wall, fence or hedge. Bulbs of various flowering times and heights can be selected for the border, placing the tallest at the back. Even narrow borders under a wall or in front of a garden summerhouse or shed will provide good sites for shorter-stemmed bulbs.

In borders where shrubs and evergreens are planted, bulbs provide attractive colour. Most of them will be enjoying the partial shade; indeed, many flowers last longer because they are not in direct sun throughout the day.

There is no doubt that, whether planted formally or informally, bulbs can make a delightful colour picture in the garden. Excepting in the case

Above *An informal border of bright spring flowers.* **Right** *Bright yellow tulips make an ideal contrast for the stately, almost black, La Tulipe Noire.*

of bulbs used for border edging, spring, summer and autumn-flowering bulbs all look best when planted in groups, which can be as small as five, although up to a dozen or more of each variety or mixture produce the boldest displays.

Fortunately, in the garden, even if we make mistakes regarding exact colour tones the whole picture is not spoiled. One reason is that the foliage of the bulbs takes away some of the colour clashes that could occur because of a wrong choice of varieties. The question of placement also comes into the finished picture; this concerns not only colour but height, size of flowers, background and environment.

Where the background to a prominent border consists of flowering shrubs, one should aim for both harmony and contrasts. It is not only the background that should be considered, for it is not difficult to

visualize the effect in spring of, for example, mauve or blue aubrietas used as a ground cover for yellow tulips; or white arabis showing up scarlet or crimson tulips; or blue forget-me-nots or muscari as an undercover for orange or yellow tulips. The dark-coloured tulip, La Tulipe Noire, can be used as a background or contrast to white, yellow or bronze-yellow tulips. In large borders tulips or other spring-flowering bulbs can be placed in irregular drifts running into each other so that as the observer walks or looks along the border, the colour is constantly changing. A few bulbs of the same colour tones could be planted at intervals throughout the border, in order to connect the various groups and provide a sense of continuity.

The shrub border itself often provides little colour in spring and the planting of spring-flowering bulbs will make up for that. Where there

are low-growing shrubs or where any kind of ground cover is used, small bulbs such as crocuses or winter aconites are best placed near the front of the border.

Clumps of narcissus and tulip species fit in well with shrubs and muscari, Heavenly Blue, makes widespread splashes of colour. In situations where the soil does not become dry, a good display in spring and early summer can be given by groups of erythroniums (dog's tooth violets) with their reflexed petals and leaves often beautifully marked. Other subjects are bluebells, snowdrops, ornithogalums (Star of Bethlehem) and *Fritillaria meleagris*, while the larger shrub border could contain a few lilies, including *Lilium pardalinum*, *L. martagon*, *L. canadense*, *L. rubellum* and *L. superbum*. In autumn hardy cyclamen, *Sternbergia lutea* and crocus species will ensure a continuation of colour.

CHAPTER 4

Hardy Bulbs for all Seasons

Whatever the size of the garden or other growing ground there are species and varieties to bring colour and beauty to every part. The following alphabetical list details many that are well known; it also includes some that are uncommon yet reliable for general culture.

Acidanthera

They are closely related to gladiolus and require similar treatment. The corms should be planted in early May 7.5 cm (3 in) deep, preferably in porous soil containing peat or leaf mould and in a sheltered, sunny position. They flower from July onwards, the corms being lifted once the foliage has withered. *A. bicolor* has scented, pure white flowers, blotched purple, on 60 cm (2 ft) stems. The kind generally known as *murielae* has the same features, but is even more attractive and reliable.

Allium

This is a large genus very diverse in form, height and colour. The many species are distributed over various parts of the world including Europe, Asia, North Africa and North America. Most grow readily in good, well-drained soil and, once established, they increase freely both by offsets and self-sown seeds. The majority have wide leaves. In early summer all produce strong stems at the top of which are well-made umbels of six-petalled flowers, which open flat in the sun. They belong to the onion family, but the scent is only noticeable when the leaves or bulbs are bruised. Among the interesting species are the following:

A. albopilosum which grows up to 60 cm (2 ft) high, and has large umbels of starry, shiny, violet-blue flowers which form into a ball-like shape;

A. beesianum, 23 to 30 cm (9 to 12 in), purplish blue;

A. caeruleum (*A. azureum*), 30 to 60 cm (1 to 2 ft), rich sky blue;

A. karataviense, 15 to 20 cm (6 to 8 in), has broad, glaucous leaves and dense umbels of white or faintly pink flowers;

A. moly, 30 cm (1 ft), is a well-known species with yellow flowers in compact umbels; often known as Golden Garlic it is inclined to be invasive (to prevent this, lift and divide the clumps every three years);

A. neapolitanum, 20 to 30 cm (8 to 12 in), white, does well in pots;

A. ostrowskianum, 20 to 30 cm (8 to 12 in), pink or purplish pink.

A. rosenbachianum, 60 to 75 cm (2 to 2½ ft), rose-purple;

A. sphaerocephalum, 30 to 60 cm (1 to 2 ft), dark purple.

Alstroemeria

These are tuberous rooted perennials of beauty and elegance, named in honour of a Swedish botanist. They are sometimes known as Peruvian Lilies. From June onwards the leafy stems bear umbels of richly coloured,

The decorative heads of Allium rosenbachianum, one of the onion family, are seen here against the handsome foliage of Hosta sieboldiana glauca.

The delicate alstroemerias or Peruvian Lilies are ideal for cutting and flower arranging.

funnel-shaped flowers. A deeply-moved, well-drained, but not dry, soil is required. Leaf mould or peat are useful additions. *A. chilensis* varies from white to cream, yellow and pink. *A. pelegrina* is clear pink. *A. psittacina* has crimson petals, tipped green. The *A. ligtu* hybrids embrace exquisite colours including pink, flame, yellow and orange.

Amaryllis belladonna

Usually known as the Belladonna Lily this is a native of South Africa. It is a charming, autumn-flowering bulb producing pale pink, funnel-shaped flowers on 60 to 75 cm (2 to 2½ ft) stems before the leaves develop. They bloom best when established, especially if mulched with decayed manure, or if bone meal is applied to the surface soil and lightly pricked in during spring. In frosty weather, a little straw or bracken should be placed on the soil covering the bulbs. There are several selected forms available including Hathor, white; Kewensis, deep pink; and Parkeri, vigorous growing, deep pink.

Anemone

This large family contains plants of very different appearance with either tuberous or rhizomatous roots, producing most delightful spring flowers. It includes:

A. blanda has blue, mauve, pink or white flowers on 13 to 15 cm (5 to 6 in) stems in early spring.

A. coronaria, the poppy anemone, is widely grown in the garden; it has, with other species, produced a series of hybrids with large flowers on 15 to 38 cm (6 to 15 in) stems in many bright colours, in single, semi-double and double forms. Especially attractive are the de Caen or Giant French forms in mixture or named varieties and the St. Brigid or semi-doubles.

A. fulgens has brilliant scarlet, single flowers on 23 to 38 cm (9 to 15 in) stems and there is a semi-double form.

A. nemorosa can sometimes be found growing wild. The white, often flushed mauve, flowers, appear on 15 to 20 cm (6 to 10 in) stems during March and April. Once established in peaty soil, the little rhizomes soon spread. There are several named forms such as Robinsoniana, lavender blue; and Royal Blue, deep blue. Propagation is by division or by seed.

Anemones thrive in fairly rich soil that does not dry out. Peat, leaf mould and loam can be added to make sandy soil suitable. By planting at different times and giving cloche protection, the flowering period can be extended.

Anomatheca (see Lapeirousia)

Arum Lily (see Zantedeschia)

Babiana

This genus of South African corms is so named because it is readily eaten by baboons. There are up to a dozen species but few are in general cultivation. The coated corms should be planted in autumn 7.5 cm (3 in) deep in sandy soil and in a sunny position. In severe winters a light surface covering of straw or bracken will provide extra protection. They flower from May onwards, although if corms are kept in a cool, dry place and planted in spring, colour can be had in August. They make excellent pot plants grown in the same way as freesias.

B. disticha has pale blue flowers on 20 cm (10 in) stems and *B. plicata* is similar but lilac-mauve. The finest species is *B. stricta*, 30 cm (1 ft) high, which has blue, lilac, pale yellow or crimson forms. Some of these have been named, one of the most brilliant being *rubro cyanea*, 10 to 15 cm (4 to 6 in), whose deep blue flowers have a red centre.

Brodiaea

This name covers a number of small-flowering plants known at various times under other names. Most are hardy, although at their best in warmer districts, where they usually increase well by bulblets. They look effective when grown in groups. The flowers are produced in umbels on stems varying in height.

B. ida-maia is known as the Californian or Floral Firecracker. When established, it produces ten or more flowers in early summer on 60 to 75 cm (2 to 2½ ft) stems, the bright crimson petals being tipped yellow. It is sometimes listed under the name brevoortia. *B. laxa* has violet-blue umbels on 75 cm (2½ ft) stems and is summer-flowering. *B. pulchella* is also blue, but shorter growing. *B. uniflora*. Once known as milla, this has now been classed by botanists as *Ipheion uniflorum*.

Bulbocodium vernum

This is the only species in the genus. It is of crocus-like appearance. It can be grown in the same way as crocuses, light soil and a sheltered position being an advantage. In fact, there are only minor botanical differences distinguishing it from the crocus and it is closely related to both merendera and colchicum. The flowers vary slightly in colour including reddish violet-purple, most with a white base and strap-shaped leaves. It is a useful subject for the rock garden or front of the border.

Camassia

Often known by the North American name of quamash, this small genus is related to the scillas. The bulbs should be planted about 7.5 cm (3 in) deep in autumn, preferably in moist but well-drained soil. A sunny or partially shaded position is suitable. Flowering in June and July, they

The tall, profusely flowering Camassia leichtlinii will flourish in sun or shade.

grow well in the border, the rock garden, beside pools or in the 'wild' garden.

C. *cusickii* grows 60 to 90 cm (2 to 3 ft) high, its star-shaped, light blue flowers being borne in racemes. C. *esculenta* is the best known, its rich blue flowers appearing on strong 75 cm (2½ ft) stems. It has a light blue form. C. *leichtlinii* is variable in colour, the blue, purple, cream or white flowers developing on 75 to 90 cm (2½ to 3 ft) stems. C. *quamash* would appear to be the same as C. *esculenta*. Propagation is by offsets.

Cardiocrinum

For long regarded as a lilium, this is now listed as a separate genus. A good subject for shrubberies and woodland areas, it should be planted shallowly in lime free soil. C. *giganteum* is the finest species producing in July 2.40 to 3 m (8 to 10 ft) stems with up to 18 trumpet-shaped, white flowers marked red on the inside. After flowering the bulbs die but not before producing offsets.

Chionodoxa

These early spring-flowering, easily grown, hardy bulbs flourish in full sun and a well-drained position. Suitably named Glory of the Snow, they are most effective when planted in patches. They should be left for three or four years before lifting and dividing after the foliage has died down. Excellent for borders, rock gardens and woodland edges, they can also be grown indoors in pots.

C. *gigantea* has gentian-blue flowers, each with a white eye. C. *luciliae* produces bright blue flowers with a clear, minute centre on 10 to 15 cm (4 to 6 in) stems, while C. *sardensis*, 20 cm (8 in), is porcelain-blue with a very small white centre. All last well when cut and are excellent for miniature arrangements.

Colchicum

These produce larger and more spectacular flowers than the Autumn Crocus, for which they are often mistaken. They show their blooms in later summer and autumn before the leaves develop and are known as 'naked ladies'. The large leaves are showy and prominent and this is why the tubers must be carefully sited, especially as the foliage persists until early summer. Plant them among dwarf shrubs, around shrub roses or in grass which does not need early cutting. Planting time is July. Of the best known species, C. byzantinum is pale rosy lilac; C. giganteum, rosy purple; while C. speciosum, rosy carmine, and its white form, C. s. album, produce tulip-like flowers. There are several hybrids such as Lilac Wonder and Violet Queen and Lilac Wonder and Violet Queen with tessellated blooms, as well as some less common winter and early spring-flowering species.

Crinum powellii

This is a late summer-flowering bulbous plant producing strap-shaped leaves and large lily-like white to rosy pink trumpets on 60 to 90 cm (2 to 3 ft) stems. There are several less common species. They should be planted in a warm, sunny position in good soil and left undisturbed for some years. A surface covering of bracken during very severe weather is helpful.

Crocosmia

A small genus of plants, closely related to the tritonias, which includes species well known as montbretias. The long, pointed leaves combine with the attractive flower spikes to make a valuable garden plant, providing first class cut flowers. The corms flourish in deep, well-drained loamy soil, containing leaf mould. Excepting in the case of the smaller-flowering montbretia which is hardy, they should be planted in early March and lifted and stored like gladiolus, preferably keeping them in trays of slightly moist peat or sandy soil.

C. crocosmiiflora is the common montbretia, growing about 60 cm (2 in) with panicles of yellow or orange flowers. From these have come the less hardy Earlham hybrids in named varieties.

C. masonorum has reddish orange flowers and is best grown in a warm border or frame. C. pottsii is the same as Tritonia pottsii, the 1.20 m (4 ft) stems producing orange-red flowers.

Crocus

This is one of the best known and favourite bulbous subjects. There are scores of species and varieties of which the flowering times cover many months. The autumn species bloom from August to November followed by those that flower from December to February, the next flowering group showing colour in February and March. These are succeeded in turn by the large-flowering Dutch varieties.

They are not particular as to soil so long as it contains feeding matter, and does not remain wet. Of the autumn-flowering species which need planting in July and August, C. speciosus, mauve- to lavender-blue and its named varieties are most reliable. Others include C. kotschyanus (zonatus), rosy lilac; C. longiflorus,  rosy lilac; C. medius, bluish mauve; C. salzmannii, rosy lilac; and C. sativus, the Saffron Crocus, rosy purplish mauve. Winter-flowering species include C. chrysanthus, yellowish orange, with deep markings and its many hybrids; C. imperati, yellowish buff, shaded purple; and C. tomasinianus, mauvish blue.

The early spring-flowering species take in C. sieberi, deep mauve; C. susianus or 'Cloth of Gold', golden yellow; striped brown; C. versicolor picturatus or 'Cloth of Silver', white, feathered purple; and C. biflorus argenteus, scented lilac blooms on a cream ground.

The large-flowered or Dutch crocuses should be planted from September onwards. They like the sun and can be left for some years to become established. Dry sunny conditions are needed during the resting period. Varieties available include Enchantress, soft blue; Large Yellow; Remembrance, violet blue; grandiflorus, purple; Striped Beauty, blue and white; and Vanguard, silvery lilac.

Above Crinum powellii alba *flowers from July to September.* **Right** Cyclamen hederaefolium (neapolitanum) *thrives under trees.*

Cyclamen

These distinct plants with fleshy corm-like tubers always attract attention. The long-stemmed leaves are more or less rounded heart-shaped, the flower petals being sharply reflexed. There are three divisions in this genus: (1) the autumn-flowering; (2) the winter- and spring-flowering, both of which are hardy; and (3) *Cyclamen persicum* which needs greenhouse or indoor treatment.

The hardy species should be planted from July onwards in good fibrous loam and leaf mould with a sprinkling of lime. They should be covered with 37 mm (1½in) of soil and can be planted at the base of

trees, a wall or at the front of the border.

Autumn-flowering species include C. *cilicium*, light pink, small green leaves with silvery zone; C. *europaeum*, deep carmine; and C. *neapolitanum*, rosy pink, marbled leaves.

Winter and spring-flowering are C. *coum*, crimson, rose or white; C. *orbiculatum*, pink, silvery foliage; C. *pseudibericum*, purplish pink, variegated foliage; and C. *repandum*, producing lilac-pink flowers in April and May, silvery marked foliage.

Cyclamen persicum can be seen at its best from October to April.

The majority of plants are raised from seed sown in August or September and grown in warmth with-

out a rest for flowering about fifteen months after sowing; they can, however, also be sown in warmth in February. The plants should be raised under cool conditions and the seedlings moved to small pots and then to bigger sizes of pot as growth proceeds. The tubers should be just exposed so that moisture does not settle on the top surface. The tubers do not divide.

Feed with liquid manure, avoid over watering and always remove faded leaves and flowers without leaving a stub to decay. There are numerous strains in separate colours and mixtures including those with frilled and scented flowers and some with silvery zoned foliage.

Daffodil (see Narcissus)

Dahlia

While dahlia tubers can be planted directly into their flowering positions from early May onwards, the best plan is to place the tubers in boxes or pots of moist, peaty soil, in a temperature around 15 deg.C (60°F). Subsequently, gradually harden off these growing plants for putting in the open ground in late May or early June.

The planting positions should be prepared early by thoroughly digging and working in well-rotted manure or good compost. The taller varieties will need supports and the flowering period is from August until frost blackens the foliage, when the tubers should be lifted, dried and stored in a frost-proof place. Some of the shoots from tubers can

be taken as cuttings, while seed, particularly from the dwarf bedding types, can be sown thinly in seed compost during February and March in a temperature of 15 to 18 deg.C (60 to 65°F).

Give all plants plenty of room; plant the tall kinds 90 cm (3 ft) apart, down to 45 cm (18 in) for the dwarf bedders.

Among the most popular types of double flowers are:

Anemone-flowered, having blooms with one or more outer rings of flattened ray florets surrounding a dense group of tubular florets and not showing a disc.

Collerette. A single outer ring of flat florets with a ring of smaller florets (the collar).

Decorative. These can be giant, large, medium or small-flowering. All are double with flattish, bluntly pointed petals.

Cactus. The fully double blooms in

giant, large, medium and small sizes have narrow, pointed, straight petals.

Semi-cactus. Similar to the cactus type, these have broader petals.

Ball dahlias. The fully double flowers are ball-shaped or slightly flattened.

Pompom. These have small globe-shaped flowers. Apart from the single bedding types, there are several smaller types, such as the thin-petalled orchid group and the miniatures, growing only 30cm (1ft) high.

Endymion

This genus is better known by its popular title of Bluebells and the species are still marketed under the name of scillas, from which they

Above *Dahlias vary greatly in size, shape and colour.* **Left** *The graceful erythronium*

pale gold flowers on 5 to 10 cm (2 to 4 in) stems. *E. cilicica* is bright yellow and slightly later in flowering. *E. tubergenii* is a hybrid between *E. cilicica* and *E. hyemalis*. It has a form known as Guinea Gold with bronze tinted leaves.

Erythronium

These graceful spring–flowering tubers are available in many attractive colours. They flourish in slightly shaded positions, in humus-rich soil where they can be left undisturbed. *E. dens-canis* is the European species, the Latin (dog's tooth) referring to the shape of the bulbs and not the flowers. They bloom in March and April on 15 cm (6 in) stems, with the petals attractively reflexed. The colours are variable; they include white, pale pink, deep pinkish mauve, all with an orange-red marking at the base of the petals, with the bright green leaves heavily marbled. There are a number of selected named forms such as Rose Beauty and Snowflake. Of the American species, *E. californicum* is creamy white; *E. grandiflorum*, golden yellow; *E. hendersonii*, pale mauve; *E. revolutum* (Trout Lily), rose pink; and *E. tuolumnense*, golden yellow with yellowish green leaves. Erythroniums can be grown in pots under cool conditions.

Freesia

The corms should be potted in August or September, placing seven or eight in each 13 cm (5 in) pot of sandy loam with the top of the corm just covered. They should stand in the cold frame until growth is seen. If possible the pots should be covered with peat and any suckers removed. A temperature around 10 deg. C (50°F) from mid-December onwards will encourage good development. Thin sticks placed round the edge of the pots with a circling tie will keep the grassy foliage upright. Watch for greenfly and spray with derris as necessary. The highly perfumed *F. refracta alba*, with white flowers having a yellow blotch, was at one time the only variety which was cultivated to any extent. There are now many hybrids in separate colours. In addition, freesias can be raised from seed sown from April to June for flowers from December onwards. For this, large pots or boxes of John Innes seed compost should be used with the seeds 5 cm (2 in) apart. Germination can be helped by mixing the seed with damp peat and by sowing when there are signs of germination. Now available are freesia corms that can be planted outside in April and May.

Below *Highly scented and colourful freesias.*

have some botanical differences. They are excellent for woodlands and other semi-shaded places, although they also grow well in the sun and look lovely throughout May.

E. non scriptus (*Scilla nutans*), the English bluebell, should be planted 8 cm (3 in) deep and left to form clumps. *E. hispanicus*, the Spanish bluebell is larger, the colour varying from pale to deep blue, pale pink and white. These two species hybridize together freely (see page 73).

Eranthis

Better known as winter aconites, these tuberous rooted perennials flower in February and March. Each crown produces solitary, yellow cupshaped flowers, with leafy bracts forming a ruff or rosette below the petals. Once planted they should be left to naturalize. *E. hyemalis*, the common winter aconite, shows its

Fritillaria

This interesting family of plants varies greatly in size and colour. Among the best known is *F. meleagris*, sometimes called Snake's Head, Chequered Lily or Guinea Flower on account of its odd but attractive colours. Each leafy 15 to 20 cm (6 to 8 in) stem produces two or three squared-off, drooping bells, chequered in tones of reddish brown, greyish mauve and chartreuse. It should be planted in a semi-shaded position. A light mulching of peat kept damp during the growing season is helpful as well as a sprinkling of bone meal in autumn.

There are other dwarf species including, *F. citrina*, pale yellow; *F. pontica*, greenish rose; and *F. persica* which can reach 60 cm (2 ft) or more, a mixture of grey, green and purple.

F. imperialis (Crown Imperial) is strikingly handsome, producing in April 75 to 90 cm (2½ to 3 ft) stems bearing a tuft of leaves beneath which appears an umbel-like group of large flowers. Named varieties include *aurora*, rich orange; *lutea maxima*, yellow; and *rubra maxima*, rich burnt orange. The bulbs of this species, which emit an unpleasant smell when bruised, should be planted 10 cm (4 in) deep in a sunny situation where the soil is somewhat moist.

Galanthus

The snowdrop is one of the best known winter- and early spring-flowering subjects. Very hardy, it will come unharmed through long spells of severe, frosty weather. Occasionally the flower stems bend because of extreme cold, but they soon return to upright when temperatures rise. It grows in sunny situations and semi-shade and can often be seen exhibiting its white flowers in quite shady corners. If grown in pots, it should be kept under cool conditions. Easy to grow, it does best on heavier soils containing leaf mould or peat which remains on the moist side. Fresh manure should be avoided, although bone meal, lightly pricked into the surface soil in early autumn, is beneficial.

It spreads quickly through division and self-seeding. When clumps become too thick, they should be lifted

and divided after flowering. If planted as dry bulbs in autumn, they often take a season to become established and produce flowers.

There are several species and varieties, some being seen only rarely in gardens:

G. nivalis is the English Snowdrop which naturalizes well and is somewhat variable. The snow white flowers have just a touch of green and are on 15 cm (6 in) stems.

The double form, *G. nivalis flore pleno*, has larger globular-shaped flowers.

Other forms include *scharlokii*, large-leaved; *viridapicis*, green spotted; *atkinsii*, S. Arnott, and Straffen, all being large-flowered.

G. plicatus has broader leaves and *G. byzantinus* is vigorous.

One of the best species is *G. elwesii* which has several forms with minor botanical differences.

G. ikariae and *G. latifolius* are other attractive species.

Less usual is the autumn-flowering species *G. reginae-olgae*, which appears in early October.

Galtonia candicans

Often known as the summer hyacinth, the large bulbs produce tufts of strap-shaped leaves and strong erect 90 to 120 cm (3 to 4 ft)

Galanthus nivalis, the snowdrop. It flowers early in spring and naturalizes well.

flower spikes on which, in August and September, appear loose racemes of 15 to 20 scented, drooping, milky white bells, frequently tipped green. Sometimes known as *Hyacinthus candicans*, these bulbs like sunny, well-drained positions. A light covering of peat or leaf mould in late autumn will provide protection during bad weather. The bulbs should be planted in early spring about 13 cm (5 in) deep. They look particularly effective in groups, planted 13 cm (5 in) apart. They can be grown in pots in a cool greenhouse. The flower spikes are useful for cutting.

Gladiolus

Although this large family contains well over a hundred species, only a few are really well known. Most of us are more familiar with the large number of hybrids seen in gardens and florists shops as cut flowers. The majority of the species are of South African origin and among those that are well worth growing, and that have been used in the production of modern varieties, are the following:

G. byzantinus: summer-flowering, sometimes known as the hardy gladiolus, this can be left in the ground undisturbed. The colour is crimson-wine.

G. blandus is white, tinted pink with maroon blotch.

G. oppositiflora is white, banded red.

G. psittacinus, salmon, marked yellow.

G. nanus is dwarf, its colour varying from white to pink. The Nanus group, raised from a cross between the yellow *G. tristis* and the red *G. cardinalis*, contains named varieties such as Peach Blossom, shell pink; Spitfire, salmon orange; and The Bride, white. Early flowering and excellent for cutting and pot culture, they grow about 60 cm (2 ft) high.

Gladiolus primulinus has had a great influence on present day hybrids; it has been used to extend the colour range of the large-flowered varieties as well as the *primulinus* hybrids, which are both dainty and excellent

Well-marked Butterfly gladioli. So attractive for garden display and cutting.

for cutting and for general decorative display.

Reference to catalogues will disclose the very large number of gladiolus varieties available, not only in the sections mentioned, but in the Butterfly, Miniature and frilled or ruffled types.

While the Nanus Gladiolus can be planted in autumn or in winter in pots in the greenhouse, the others should be planted outside from late March onwards. Place the corms at least 10cm (4in) deep, otherwise the spikes may blow over during strong winds. Make sure the roots do not dry out in early summer. When cutting the spikes, two or three leaves should be left to enable the developing young corms to complete their growth.

Hermodactylus tuberosus

This is known as the Snake's Head or Mourning Iris. The narrow, tuberous root stock produces bright green, four-sided leaves and slender erect stems. In March it bears flowers with green standards and black falls. Once catalogued as *Iris tuberosa*, this plant likes a warm, dry, sunny position. Propagation is by division or seed.

Hyacinth

There are several dozen species of hyacinth, but only a few are in general cultivation. Of the dwarf types, *Hyacinthus amethystinus* is one of the loveliest. Growing 20cm (8in) high, it produces spikes of pale porcelain-blue flowers in March and April. It also has a white form. *H. azureus*, 17 to 20cm (7 to 8in), is azure-blue. *H. romanus*, better known as the Roman hyacinth, popular for early flowering in pots and bowls, produces loose spikes of whitish bells. There are now varieties in shades of pink and blue.

It is, however, *H. orientalis* which has proved to be so important, for from it have come most of the large-flowered varieties so popular for greenhouse and living room culture as well as being superb for spring bedding. It is very suitable, too, for forcing into early growth and for that prepared bulbs should be used. This is done by the trade growers giving warm treatment which favours flower bud formation but retards leaf development.

The earliest bulbs should be planted in August or September and kept in a cool dark place to form roots. Leave them there, making sure the compost does not dry out, until they are well rooted and top growth and flower bud can be seen. Unprepared bulbs take two or three weeks longer to develop, although the Roman variety will be quicker. There are dozens of named varieties in a very wide colour range, all of which will flourish in bulb fibre when grown in bowls or in loamy soil in pots. They include:

Lady Derby, Princess Margaret: pale pink.

Pink Pearl, Salmonetta: deep pink.
Jan Bos, Amsterdam: red.
City of Haarlem, Gipsy Queen: yellow.

L'Innocence, Carnegie: white.
Delft Blue, Myosotis: pale blue.
King of the Blues, Ostara: deep blue.

Amethyst: lilac-mauve.

Bulbs planted in the open ground in September or October will usually flower in April.

Ipheion

This small genus contains only one species that is well known in cultivation. This is *I. uniflorum*, known for a long time as milla and later as a brodiaea, then a triteleia. On 15cm (6in) stalks it produces white, pale lilac or pale mauve flowers in March and April. It has grass-like foliage and is quite hardy, being useful for the front of a sunny border. The bulbs can be divided once they form large clumps.

Iris

This is a very large and important family of plants which can be conveniently divided into two groups, bulbous and rhizomatous. We can refer only to a very few of the many delightful species and varieties. Most of the dwarf bulbous section are very suitable for border edging, rock gardens, naturalizing and for growing in pots. They should be planted 7 to 8cm (3 to 4in) deep in the autumn, preferably in soil containing plenty of leaf mould or peat and some lime.

Reference to bulb catalogues will reveal the wide range of other irises available.

I. bakeriana, 15cm (6in), has lilac blue flowers blotched black, and stiff, ribbed leaves.

I. danfordiae, 7.5cm (3in), has scented lemon flowers in February; the bulbs split after flowering, the offsets not blooming for at least two years.

I. histrioides major, 7.5cm (3in), is gentian-blue with white spots, flowering in March.

I. reticulata, 13 to 14cm (5 to 6in), boasts fragrant, velvety blue-purple flowers, blotched orange, from February onwards. It has a number of named hybrids including Cantab, light blue; Harmony, dark blue; Hercules, bronze; J. S. Dijt, reddish purple; and Joyce, rich blue.

I. vartani, slaty lavender and almond-scented, has a white form and is very early in flowering.

I. xiphioides is often known as the English iris although it is not a native of this country. Growing up to 60cm (2ft) it has large golden blotched, deep blue flowers from late June onwards. It is, however, the hybrids of this species that are valued in the garden. They include named varieties as well as separate colours.

I. xiphium blooms from late May onwards. It is best known as Spanish iris. Separate varieties are available including Cajanus, yellow; Hercules, blue shaded bronze; and Queen Wilhelmina, white. Dutch irises flower before the Spanish varieties. They are the result of *I. xiphium var. praecox* and *I. tingitana* crosses and have a wide colour range.

Beautiful rhizomatous iris species include *I. bucharica*, creamy white, and *I. graeberiana*, silvery mauve and rich blue. *I. persica* is greenish blue, marked purple and gold.

Ixia

Natives of South Africa and known as Corn Lilies, these are of a most graceful appearance. The colourful flowers appear on wiry 38 to 45cm (15 to 18in) stems in June and July, the narrow foliage being an added attraction. They are not fully hardy

They include:

Afterglow: orange buff.

Azurea: blue.

Bridesmaid: white.

Vulcan: scarlet, shaded orange.

Ixia viridiflora is an exciting greenish blue colour flowering earlier than the hybrids.

Ixiolirion

This small family of bulbous plants can be grown in pots or pans in a cool greenhouse, but they are mostly grown outdoors in sheltered positions and in fairly rich, well-drained soil. Amid the grey-green foliage arise slender stems up to 38 cm (15 in) high on which funnel-shaped flowers appear. Plant the bulbs in autumn or very early in spring protecting the surface soil during bad weather. *I. kolpakowskianum* has pale blue or whitish flowers in May and June, while *I. montanum*, sometimes known as *I. ledebourii* or *I. pallasii*, is rich lavender-blue.

Lapeirousia cruenta

Sometimes known as *Anomatheca cruenta*, this needs a warm, sheltered position. It can be treated in the same manner as ixias. Stems of 30 to 35 cm (12 to 14 in) are produced in summer, bearing star-like, carmine-scarlet flowers.

Leucojum

Frequently known as snowflakes and in some respects looking like large snowdrops, leucojums are suitable for growing in the border, the rock garden and for naturalizing, while they are also useful for cutting. The bulbs should be planted 8 to 10 cm (3 to 4 in) deep during September and October, in full sun or partial shade. According to species, they flower in February or in May and June. The early flowering species are scented and the best known is *L. vernum*, the Spring Snowflake, the little white bells, tipped green, appearing on 15 cm (6 in) stems.

L. aestivum, the Summer Snowflake, has umbels of green-tipped, nodding bells on 45 cm (18 in) stems, flowering in May and June. A larger form, named Gravetye, is particularly attractive.

Ixias are available in a huge variety of shades and colour combinations.

and can be given the same culture as freesias in a cool greenhouse, planting five corms in each 13 to 15 cm (5 to 6 in) pot in October. In warm districts they can be planted outdoors and given a covering of weathered ashes and bracken during severe frosts.

There are several excellent named varieties, all of which open fully in sunlight revealing a central blotch.

35

Lilium

Along with daffodils, tulips and crocuses, lilies are among the best
known and loved bulbous flowers.
With a few exceptions, most are easy
to grow, the majority thriving in
open ground in good, well-drained
soil. A few are happiest when grown
in a cold or cool greenhouse. The
stateliness and purity of many species with white or near white flowers
are well known but in recent years
very many coloured hybrids have
been brought into cultivation.

Liliums deserve a whole volume to
themselves and in the limited space
now available we can deal only
briefly with them.

Many lilies thrive in the sun, but
others prefer partial shade and are
therefore at home in the herbaceous
border or among shrubs where the
lower parts of the stem are shaded.
Good drainage is essential.

Lilies can be divided into two
groups according to their rooting systems – those that form basal roots,
and those that have additional roots
on the stem. The non-stem rooting
species should generally be planted
two and a half times the depth of the
bulb with the exceptions of *L. candidum*, for which 3 to 5 cm (1 to 2 in) is
sufficient, and of *L. testaceum*, 8 cm
(3 in). The stem rooting species
(marked with an asterisk) must be
planted deeply, 13 cm (5 in) being the
minimum. It is, therefore, important
to know to which particular rooting
system a species belongs.

Fresh manure should never be
used and it is best to avoid artificial
fertilizers when preparing the
ground. Old decayed manure, bone
meal, and hoof and horn meal are
safe, and will provide organic
feeding over a long period. There is
no real evidence to support the belief
that liliums will not grow in ground
containing lime, although some species do better in lime free soil. Popular species that grow well in cal-
careous soil include *brownii, candidum, croceum, hansonii, henryi, martagon, regale* and *testaceum.*

When buying lilies make sure the
scales are firm and plump; if they are
soft and flabby it indicates they have
been out of the ground and exposed
to the air for some time. When planting use a trowel or spade so that the
bulb can be placed in a large hole and
is not 'screwed up'.

The following is a list of a few of
the most beautiful species; many
more will be found on referring to the
catalogues of bulb specialists:

**L. auratum*, the golden rayed lily

The last named was raised by Mrs. Isabella Preston of Ottawa, while Jan de Graaf has bred many hybrids at his Oregon bulb farm.

Merendera montana

A small genus having erect, funnel-shaped, rosy lilac flowers, similar to colchicum, flowering from July to October. The growing conditions are the same as for colchicums.

Montbretia

Many of the well-known garden species and varieties have now been transferred to other genera, for example, crocosmia and tritonia. There is, however, *M. laxiflora*, with flowers of orange, copper and red shading in summer, on stems up to 60 cm (2 ft) tall. The corms increase rapidly when planted in deep, well-drained soil.

Muscari

Easy to grow, the bulbs of the grape hyacinths increase rapidly. The flowers consist of small bells, borne in dense racemes, with narrow leaves. All like sunshine.

M. armeniacum, 20 to 25 cm (8 to 10 in), has heads of azure-blue in April and May. Its forms include Cantab, pale blue; and Heavenly Blue, which is the best known.

M. botryoides is china blue and it also has a white form, *M. plumosum*.

M. comosum grows 38 cm (15 in) or more high and in June forms loose heads of purplish blue; a form known as *monstrosum*, mauvish blue, is known as the tassel or feather hyacinth.

M. flavum has yellow flower spikes 5 to 8 cm (2 to 3 in) high.

M. moschatum, the Musk hyacinth, produces in spring 13 cm (5 in) spikes of sweetly scented yellowish olive flowers.

M. racemosum, the Starch hyacinth, is well known, having 15 cm (6 in) spikes of blue flowers in May.

M. tubergenianum from Persia is known as the Oxford and Cambridge grape hyacinth because of the contrast of the dark blue flowers at the apex and the pale blue of the lower bells on the 20 cm (8 in) spikes in the early spring. It is suitable for rock gardens.

Left Lilium cardinal, *a splendid Turk's Cap hybrid, planted to give height at the back of a border.* **Above** Muscari flavum *is an unusual yellow flowering species.*

of Japan. Flowering from August onwards it produces many white scented flowers which are golden rayed and spotted crimson. It has several forms.

L. brownii, white trumpets with brown exterior; 90 to 120 cm (3 to 4 ft). July.

L. candidum, the white Madonna lily; 1.20 to 1.50 cm (4 to 5 ft). July.

L. chalcedonicum, orange-red; 90 to 120 cm (3 to 4 ft). July.

L. hansonii, yellowish orange, spotted; 1.20 to 1.50 m (4 to 5 ft), summer.

L. henryi, rich yellow; 2 m (6 ft), August to September.

L. longiflorum, the white 'florists' lily; 1 m (3 ft), forces well. This has many forms including Croft, eximium and White Queen.

L. martagon is the Turk's Cap, pinkish purple; 1 to 2 m (3 to 6 ft). It has many forms of varying heights and colours. There are several groups of hybrids.

L. pardalinum is the Panther Lily, orange-red; 2 m (6 ft). July.

L. regale, white, stained rose, purple on the exterior, fragrant; 1.50 m (5 ft). July.

L. rubellum, rosy pink, fragrant; 60 cm (2 ft). June.

L. speciosum, white, pink spots; up to 2 m (6 ft). July to September. It has many first class named forms.

L. testaceum is a natural cross between *L. candidum* and *L. chalcedonicum*, apricot yellow, spotted red; 1.50 m (5 ft), June to July.

L. tigrinum is the Tiger Lily, orange-red, spotted; 2 m (6 ft), July to September.

L. wardii, a pinkish purple martagon; up to 1.50 m (5 ft), July to August.

There are many other delightful groups of hybrid lilies such as:

Aurelian
Bellingham
Coolhurst
Green Dragon
Mid Century
Olympic
Stooke's
Preston

Left *Short-cupped, long lasting narcissus.* **Right** *Narcissus bulbocodium. The Hoop Petticoat, there are white and yellow forms.*

Narcissus

It would not be difficult to devote a whole volume to the narcissus family and there are several comprehensive books on this subject. One cannot imagine spring in the flower garden without narcissus which, of course, includes the popular trumpet daffodil. The family is divided into groups, each being distinguished by the length of the corona, cup or trumpet. These include large-cupped, small-cupped, trumpet, double, triandrus, tazetta, poeticus, jonquils and dwarf.

Large-cupped narcissi are those having a cup or corona more than one third the length of the petals. Good varieties include Carlton, golden yellow; Carbineer, yellow and orange-red; Fortune, yellow, fiery red cup; Hades, white, red cup; Ruston Pasha, yellow, red cup; and Salmon Trout, white, salmon-pink cup. Small-cupped have a corona of less than one third the length of the petals. Varieties include: Birma, pale yellow, orange-scarlet cup; Barrett Browning, white, orange-red cup and Blarney, white, salmon-pink corona.

Trumpet narcissi of quality include:

Yellow: Dutch Master, King Alfred, Golden Harvest and Unsurpassable.

Bicolor: Foresight, Preamble and Trousseau.

White: Beersheba, Cantatrice and Mount Hood.

Double daffodils of merit are Inglescombe, yellow; Mary Copeland, creamy white and orange-red; and Texas, yellow and orange-scarlet. Cheerfulness produces several sweet-scented, creamy white flowers on each stem and is valuable for early forcing. Other double varieties are N. *albus plenus odoratus*, scented, white; Irene Copeland, creamy white and apricot and N. *telemonius plenus*, the old yellow double daffodil.

Triandrus narcissi are most graceful and mostly small growing, usually with perianth segments reflected and often twisted. N. *triandrus albus* or Angel's Tears is white or creamy yellow, several flowers to a stem. It has a number of named forms such as concolor, yellow and pulchellus. Silver Chimes is a triandrus hybrid, Thalia is a larger form.

Tazetta narcissi are bunch-flowered. Among them are Geranium, white, orange-scarlet cup and Scarlet Gem, yellow and deep orange.

The poeticus section takes in the old Pheasant Eye or *recurvus*, and Actaea, both of which have white petals with a deep red eye.

Jonquils are always attractive not least because of their scent. N. *jonquilla* itself has rush-like leaves and small golden yellow cups. N. *odorus rugulosus*, the Campernelle jonquil, is larger, while Sweetness and Trevithian are very popular.

The dwarf bulbocodium varieties are attractive and useful for the rock garden, pots and pans. The species itself has given rise to a number of sub-species such as *citrinus*, lemon yellow, funnel-shaped; *conspicuus*, the yellow hoop petticoat; and *romieuxii*, lemon yellow, January flowering. The dwarf yellow trumpet daffodils are attractive and include N. *asturiensis*, a perfect miniature 5 to 10 cm (2 to 4 in) high. N. *minor* is a small rather variable bicolor, while N. *pseudonarcissus* or N. *lobularis* is a hardy yellow trumpet.

There are several autumn-flowering narcissi, none of which is particularly striking; they are chiefly of interest because they flower in September and October. N. *elegans* has greenish white petals and a pale orange cup. N. *serotinus* is white and leafless at flowering time, as is the green flowering N. *viridiflorus*.

All narcissi root early and should be planted as soon as convenient in August, although it is possible to obtain a good display from later plantings. Plant the bulbs from 8 to 13 cm (3 to 5 in) deep. They flourish in all types of soil that are well-drained and contain plenty of feeding matter. Fresh manure, however, should not be used at any time.

Nerine

Easily grown, autumn-flowering bulbs from South Africa, the funnel-shaped flowers, often with recurving petals, are carried in umbels on slender, strong stems. *N. bowdenii* will flower well in a warm border or sheltered spot. On 60 cm (2 ft) stems, it produces pale pink flowers from November onwards. 'Fenwick's variety' is a larger form. The other species flourish in the cool greenhouse growing 30 to 60 cm (1 to 2 ft) high. They include *N. filifolia*, pink; *N. flexuosa*, pink, striped red; and *N. sarniensis*, the Guernsey lily, salmon-scarlet, which has various forms and hybrids. After blooming, keep the foliage growing and dry off the bulbs in early spring. Repotting is necessary only every three or four years.

Ornithogalum

This family of plants contains species suitable for the border, the rock garden and for cutting. Most are hardy but a few need cool greenhouse culture. Any good soil suits these bulbs which look best when planted in bold groups.

O. arabicum needs a warm, sheltered spot, its pearly white flowers appearing in early summer.

O. nutans, 15 to 23 cm (6 to 9 in)

high, is silvery grey. It is best in semi-shade, and is hardy.

O. umbellatum (Star of Bethlehem) is white, striped green; good for naturalizing.

O. pyramidale is white.

O. thyrsoides is the Chincherinchee from South Africa. This has long, thickish foliage and a closely-clothed flower head of starry white on 30 to 38 cm (12 to 15 in) stems; ideal for cutting. The bulbs should be lifted in autumn.

Puschkinia scilloides

Related to both chionodoxa and scilla and needing similar growing conditions, this bulb gives a pleasing effect in spring, especially when planted in little groups. Sometimes listed as *P. libanotica* or the Lebanon or Striped Squill, the 10 to 15 cm (4 to 6 in) stems bear six or more flowers, each silvery blue petal having darker blue line markings. There is also a white form. Plant the bulbs 7.5 cm (3 in) deep. They can be grown in pots if not forced.

Ranunculus

The tuberous rooted species in this large genus are valued by all gardeners. Most, if not all, come from 'R. asiaticus. All thrive in good soil which

Above *Paeony-flowered ranunculus come in many colours.* **Right** *Scilla sibirica. It grows well in rock gardens, borders and pots.*

does not dry out and are best planted in sunny, unexposed positions. They flower most freely once they become established. Most are best planted, claws downwards, in the early spring, though the Turban group can be planted in autumn. There are three main groups, each name of which is descriptive of the appearance of the flowers – Giant French, Double Turban and Paeony flowered. The colour range is extensive. The flowering times extend from spring to summer.

Scilla

These are pretty spring-flowering bulbous plants having the common name of Squill. They flourish in almost any kind of well-drained soil, in full sun or partial shade. They increase quickly when grown in plenty of humus. Excellent for the front of the border and rock garden, they can be naturalized in short grass or between shrubs. The best display is obtained where bulbs are planted in groups.

S. bifolia has 20 cm (8 in) spikes of gentian-blue; *S. sibirica* carries Prussian blue bells on 8 to 10 cm (3 to 4 in) stems, as does the white form. The most showy is the named variety Spring Beauty which is twice the size of *S. sibirica*. *S. tubergeniana* has delicate soft blue flowers from February onwards. Scillas can be grown in pots or bowls indoors.

Snowdrops (see Galanthus)

Sparaxis

Sometimes known as the Harlequin Flower because of its bright sprays of cup-shaped flowers of many colours, these little gems grow about 20 cm (8 in) tall and flower from June to August. The bulbs should be planted 5 cm (2 in) deep in well-drained soil

from mid-April onwards. They thrive in warm, sunny situations and the bulbs should be lifted after the foliage has died down. They should be stored safely for the winter.

Sternbergia

These hardy bulbs do well in any good, well-moved soil in the border, rock garden or on well-drained banks. The long-necked bulbs produce strap-shaped leaves and funnel-shaped flowers. *S. lutea* shows its crocus-like, golden yellow flowers during August and September, the leaves often developing after the flowers. It has both smaller and larger forms. Much less common are *S.*

colchiciflora, pale yellow and scented; and *S. fischeriana*, 10 to 15 cm (4 to 6 in), spring-flowering.

Tigridia pavonia

Known as the Tiger Flower, the flowers embrace some wonderful colourings and markings. All are spotted and attractively marbled, the contrasting colours of the cup and petals being most remarkable. Bulbs often become available in winter, but should be kept in a frost-proof place, stored in slightly moist peat for planting in sandy soil in early April. They flower from July onwards, each bloom lasting only a day before being quickly replaced by others.

Tulip

Colourful aristocrats of the spring, these are among the most popular of bulbous flowers. They come in many massive, stately forms. The colour range is extremely wide including plain and 'broken' colours, striped, streaked, tinged and shaded, and they include pure white and almost black.

Easy to cultivate, the bulbs should be planted in October or November, placing them 11 to 13 cm (4 to 5 in) deep, preferably in an open position. They are tolerant of a wide range of soils provided that drainage is good. The tulip species are most attractive and can be left to naturalize and increase. It is advisable to gather the flower petals and stems once they have faded. This lessens the possibility of 'tulip fire' (see page 75). We can only mention a few of the species; others will be found described in bulb catalogues.

Tulipa acuminata is distinct because of its yellow or red 5 to 8 cm (2 to 3 in) spidery, twisted petals.

T. batalinii is creamy yellow on 15 to 20 cm (6 to 10 in) stems.

T. clusiana, the Lady Tulip, has pinkish crimson streaks on the outside of white petals.

T. eichleri, 38 cm (15 in), is scarlet.

T. fosteriana, vermilion scarlet, has several forms.

T. greigii is also a distinct vermilion scarlet with various exterior markings.

T. kaufmanniana, 15 to 38 cm (6 to 15 in) has white or yellowish petals with various crimson markings.

T. praestans carries several scarlet flowers on 20 to 30 cm (10 to 12 in) stems.

T. saxatilis is pinkish magenta.

T. silvestris, 30 cm (1 ft) is yellowish green.

T. tarda (dasystemon), 15 cm (6 in), is yellowish green, marked red. The large-flowering tulips are divided into sections including the Single Earlies flowering from late March. There are scores of varieties varying in height from 30 to 40 cm (12 to 16 in). They are excellent for growing in pots and bowls as well as in the garden. Among the best are Bellona, yellow; Brilliant Star, scarlet; Couleur Cardinal, crimson; General de Wet, orange, stippled scarlet; Ibis, deep rose; and Prince of Austria, orange-red, scented.

Double tulips follow a few days later, growing from 25 to 30 cm (10 to 12 in) high. They are excellent for window boxes and other outdoor containers. They include Electra, cherry red; Maréchal Niel, yellowish orange; Orange Nassau, orange-scarlet; Peach Blossom, rosy pink; Mr. Van der Hoef, yellow; and Schoonoord, pure white.

Mendel tulips have large single cups on 40 to 60 cm (16 to 24 in) stems. Excellent for forcing, some varieties are edged with a contrasting colour. They include Apricot Beauty, salmon, tinged red; Athlete, white; Olga, violet-red, edged white; and Ruby Red, scarlet.

Triumph tulips succeed the Mendels; they have strong stems of the same height, are weather-resistant and have cone-shaped flowers. Albury is currant red; Dreaming Maid, violet, edged white; Golden Melody, yellow; Kees Nelis, red, edged yellow; Orient Express, vermilion; and Topscore, geranium-red. Raised from Single Early and Darwin varieties they are ideal for exposed garden positions and can easily be forced.

Darwin tulips have been popular throughout the century. The large-cupped flowers are squared off at the top and base of the petals, with strong and sturdy 55 to 80 cm (22 to 32 in) stems. Flowering from late April onwards, they are superb in beds and borders and can be grouped effectively among shrubs and evergreens and also grown in pots. First class varieties include: Aristocrat, purplish violet; Bleu Aimable, violet-purple, shaded blue; Clara Butt, soft rose; Cordell Hull, blood-red, flaked white; Queen of Bartigons, salmon-pink; Sweet Harmony, pale yellow, edged white; and Zwanenburg, white. Darwin hybrid tulips are the result of crosses between Darwin varieties and *T. fosteriana* Red Emperor, orange-

Above *Tulipa greigii*. A brilliantly coloured dwarf tulip. **Right** *Tulipa viridiflora*, Green Knight. An attractive cottage tulip.

scarlet; Gudoshnik, yellow; and Oxford, red.

Cottage tulips are May-flowering. Their heights range from 25 to 32 cm (10 to 16 in) with an extremely wide colour range. Certain varieties once known as Breeder tulips are now included in the Cottage section as are the lily-flowered varieties, which have reflexing petals and wiry stems of 30 to 40 cm (12 to 16 in).

Rembrandt tulips have petals with feathered or flamed 'broken' colours, making them excellent for flower decoration.

Parrot tulips, too, are unusual: their large flowers have laciniated petals creating a fringed or waved effect. They grow up to 30 cm (1 ft) high and should be planted in sheltered positions. Colours include violet, purplish black, yellow, white

and soft rose, blotched green.

Tulipa viridiflora is an unusual greenish tulip and from it have come a series of interesting hybrids all in various shades of green and with striking pointed petals.

Watsonia

Closely related to the gladiolus with similar corms and sword-shaped leaves, watsonias are not fully hardy though it is possible to grow some outdoors in mild, sheltered situations. There are several dozen species, but only very few are in general cultivation. These like sun and well-drained soil. *W. ardernei*, 90 cm (3 ft), pure white, is the best known. *W. meriana*, 20 to 75 cm (8 to 30 in) is salmon, mauvish pink, and *W. pyramidata* (rosea), 1.5 m (5 ft), rose red.

Winter Aconites (see Eranthis)

Zantedeschia

This is the official name for the plants, which have long been called calla and richardia or, more commonly, Arum Lilies, although they are not true lilies.

The tubers can be potted from the end of July for flowering from December onwards. August plantings are often made to give flowers during March and April for the Easter period. A minimum winter temperature of 15 deg. C (60°F) is needed.

Z. aethiopica is white, and well-known for its use in flower decorations. *Z. elliottiana* is yellow and distinguished by silvery blotches on its foliage and *Z. rehmannii* is purplish pink and has red and scarlet forms.

CHAPTER 5

Naturalizing Bulbs

There are occasions when it is possible to provide interest and pleasure by planting bulbs informally in grassland, woodland, under trees and shrubs, in orchards, on banks or slopes and in remote corners of the garden.

How to display

Naturalization is a delightful, labour-saving way of growing bulbs. The system requires little initial labour or aftercare. No annual cultivation or staking are needed and the only weeding required is the removal of unusually vigorous weeds or any that harbour pests.

Ignore the usual spacing rules and instead of making formal groups, plant the bulbs at the usual depth in irregular clumps. Once established, they will fend for themselves and multiply over the years as they do in nature.

If there is to be an annual display of colour, one essential requirement is that the grass is not cut until the leaves of the bulbs have died down. Some careful selection of varieties is necessary, therefore, since in the case of various bulbs (narcissi, for instance) the foliage often remains green until the end of June. Many bulbs will grow happily on grassy banks and slopes as well as on rough areas, but it is unwise to plant them on lawns which are mown early.

When planting in new lawns in the early autumn, place the bulbs at their usual planting depth. In the case of established lawns or other grassland, either lift a section of turf or use the special bulb planters which take out a 'cup' of turf and soil. A little bone meal sprinkled at the bottom of the holes will provide long-lasting feeding material.

If planting among shrubs or under trees, remember that some are evergreen and some deciduous. Taller-growing bulbs such as liliums, camassias and galtonias look well among evergreens, which act as a foil to the flowering display.

Naturalized bulbs should be regarded as permanent residents of the garden and its surroundings. It is, therefore, essential that the soil in which they are planted is deep, fertile and well-drained. If, after a number of years of multiplying and creating attractive patterns and colour pictures, the bulbs become too overcrowded, some can be lifted after the foliage has died down, and be separated for size before replanting. When planting bulbs in groups of half dozens rather than hundreds, it is wise to relate them closely to some particular feature, such as a tree or shrub.

What to plant

For a spring display, blue muscari will look well under bright yellow forsythia or around chaenomeles (sometimes known as japonica). Snowdrops in quantity scattered around dark, evergreen shrubs show up well. Small-growing daffodils combined with the light blue flowers of chionodoxas or puschkinias are

Fritillaria meleagris. The Snake's Head fritillary with its chequered, bell-shaped flowers looks spectacular in large numbers.

46

most attractive, whilst daffodils also look superb growing under flowering cherries or the lighter coloured foliage of trees and shrubs.

Bright yellow winter aconites look well in quantity beneath the lower branches of the winter-bronzed foliage of mahonias or the shorter-growing berberis. In shady or partially shaded positions, there are several good

hardy anemones that produce a carpet of colour. These include the lovely blue Anemone appenina and Anemone blanda in shades of blue, pink and white. Chionodoxa luciliae produces its blue flowers early in the year. It is a subject that seeds freely, producing rapidly expanding colonies with some variation in the shades of blue.

On a moist and partially shaded site, camassias naturalize well; in fact, they never attain their full size on hot or dry sandy soils. Plant the bulbs in autumn about 10cm (4in) deep and leave them undisturbed for some years. There are several good

Anemone blanda flowers in early spring and is excellent for naturalizing, or for rock gardens.

species such as *C. esculenta* (sometimes known as *C. quamash*), its starlike flowers showing in June and July on stems 60 to 90 cm (2 to 3 ft) high. It is variable in colour, from white to ultramarine blue.

Fritillaria meleagris, the Snake's Head or Guinea Flower, grows well in damp meadows, in any moist garden soil or in open woodland. On 20 to 25 cm (8 to 10 in) stems, it produces mottled flowers which look particularly attractive in the garden under the spreading branches of cotoneasters. In grassland, too, fritillarias are most attractive.

The common bluebell, *Scilla nutans*, which is now officially known as *Endymion non scriptus*, multiplies rapidly when naturalized in woody and shady areas, although it also flowers well in full sun. For the finest display the bulbs should be planted in quantity up to 10 cm (4 in) deep in the autumn, the flowers appearing from April to June.

Erythronium dens-canis, Dog's Tooth Violet or Pagoda Flower, will always attract attention in grassland or in shrubberies.

The Spring Snowflake, *Leucojum vernum*, also naturalizes well in dampish soil. It produces little white bells tipped with green from early February onwards. For crocuses, the large-flowered hybrids are showy in many shades of blue, white, striped and yellow. The yellows are best planted in separate groups.

There are various crocus species which are most suitable for the rock garden or woodlands where the grass does not grow tall, e.g. *C. sieberi, C. susianus, C. versicolor picturatus* and *C. biflorus argenteus*.

Several of the narcissus species naturalize well and *N. bulbocodium*, in various shades of cream and yellow, is seen at its best in damp meadowland. The so-called Lent Lilies, *N. pseudonarcissus* and *N. lobularis*, are often regarded as wild daffodils. They stand up to rough weather and can occasionally be found growing in old woodland and grassland areas. They have golden yellow trumpets with paler cream petals; they flower about fourteen days before the larger varieties.

Elegant trumpet narcissi are among the earliest of spring heralds in the bulb garden.

There are a number of larger daffodils that are a success in grassland although they are mostly the older, shorter-growing varieties not now as readily available as in the past. They include Golden Spur, a yellow trumpet variety; Carlton, a popular large-cupped yellow narcissus; while the various forms of the Pheasant's Eye narcissus look specially good planted on a large scale, as does the old-fashioned, golden yellow double variety Van Sion.

Hardy cyclamen are easily grown and will thrive in shady positions at the base of walls or fences, under trees and on hedge banks and slopes. There are species that flower from autumn to spring. The corms should be planted from July onwards and covered with 5 to 8 cm (2 to 3 in) of soil. Among the best are *C. neapolitanum* or *C. orbiculatum* with rose-pink flowers in autumn before the mottled foliage develops and *C. europaeum*, scented carmine rose, blooming in autumn. *C. coum* in pink, red and white forms, appears in winter and in April, *C. repandum* shows its crimson flowers, well set off by its handsome mottled foliage.

There are some liliums that are suitable for planting in woodland areas. They need some sun and should be planted where the soil is in reasonably good condition. One of the best for this purpose is *L. martagon*, the Turk's Cap lily, in its various forms. The bulbs should be planted up to 15 cm (6 in) deep in good soil containing some leaf mould or lime. Left to become established, they will increase by means of offsets and the seeds which fall to the ground and germinate freely. Seedlings take some years to reach flowering size. This species varies in height from 1 to 2 m (3 to 6 ft) and in colour from light purple to purplish pink, spotted with various purple shades. The many dark green leaves are arranged in whorls. *L. martagon* is rather unpleasant in smell and this makes it unsuitable for growing near the house. This applies in varying degrees to its forms with red, white and spotted flowers.

L. pardalinum, the Leopard lily,

grows from 1 to 2 m (3 to 6 ft) or more high, producing heavily spotted, orange-red flowers. The Bellingham hybrids in named varieties with heavily spotted, yellow or orange flowers, on 2 to 3 m (6 to 9 ft) stems, are most vigorous in growth. The little pink *L. rubellum*, up to 60 cm (2 ft) high, produces its fragrant blooms in June; sometimes difficult to establish, it does not like wet rooting conditions in winter.

Cardiocrinum giganteum produces a rosette of dark green foliage at the base of the stems which may be anything from 2 to 3.5 m (6 to 10 ft) high. The funnel-shaped, white fragrant flowers are about 15 cm (6 in) long, with reddish purple stains on the exterior. After flowering the bulb divides into smaller bulbs which take

up to four years to flower. Because of its size, this woodland subject can only be grown where there is plenty of room. It likes shallow planting where there is little lime but it is not suitable for sandy soil or hot, dry positions.

Fertilizers

Naturalized bulbs can be fed by lightly working in a dusting of bone meal around the bulb planted area; if necessary it can be spread directly on the grass. Alternatively, where bulbs are in grassland or under trees and shrubs, they can be helped while dormant by an application of peat or leaf mould. Naturalized bulbs will continue for years, multiplying and creating new garden pictures.

Left Lilium pardalinum. *The Leopard lily grows well in semi-shade or full sun.* **Right** *Daffodils increase freely in grassland.*

CHAPTER 6

Container Grown Bulbs

A visitor to European countries such as France, Belgium, Holland, Italy and Switzerland cannot fail to be impressed by the abundance of window boxes, pots, vases and other containers filled with luxuriant hyacinths, crocuses, tulips and a wide range of other spring flowers. At other times of the year different types of bulbs occupy these containers. They are sometimes combined with annual plants or dwarf shrubby subjects.

It is an aspect of flower growing which is gaining in popularity in Britain. Today the terrace, the verandah and the patio are increasingly becoming places of leisure where one can stand or fix attractive boxes, vases and pots in which to grow bulbous plants. Containers filled with bulbs or the fleshy-rooted agapanthus also look attractive on steps, in doorways, in selected places on lawns or at the base of bare posts supporting sectional roofs over patios, etc.

Indoor displays

Their amazing adaptability and their natural flair for looking at home in so many places make bulbs particularly suitable for indoor display.

Growing plants and bulbs in containers is a distinctive form of gardening and one of its attractions is that containers can often be moved around and can be filled with different species or varieties so that there is a change of display each season.

Changing window boxes and vases can be made easy by planting them in a liner which can be lifted out as soon as the occupants lose their colour. Liners are usually made of metal, including aluminium, or pottery. These are made slightly smaller so that they slot into the window box. The replacement (i.e. later-flowering) bulbs are planted in a second liner. After the flowers in the first liner have faded, they can be lifted out and the replacement put in position. The first planting should be kept watered until the foliage discolours or can be placed straight into the open ground.

Soil and fertilizers

The type of soil or compost is important but one must first ensure that drainage is suitable. Containers with drainage holes must have crocks or pieces of broken pots placed at the bottom. This not only ensures that excess water can run away but prevents the soil packing down and becoming airless. If this should happen, the roots would gradually decay and growth be spoiled. A simple compost for most bulbs can be made up from four parts loamy soil, one part peat (or leaf mould) and one part silver sand; to this should be added a good sprinkling of bone meal or decayed manure. Seaweed fertilizer also encourages good unforced growth. The ready-made John Innes composts are very suitable and can be bought in small quantities. There are, of course, a number of other soil mixtures very suitable for bulb culture which can readily be bought in both small and large quantities.

Begonia pendula is first class for hanging baskets in greenhouse or patio.

Planting

Depth of planting is important and this will depend on the subjects being grown. Obviously the larger daffodils and taller tulips will need to be placed much deeper than the smaller-growing bulbs such as scillas, muscaris, crocuses and chionodoxas. This means that larger containers should be used for the bigger bulbs, since daffodils and tulips should be covered by at least 7.5 to 10 cm (3 to 4 in) of soil. Shallow planting can easily lead to the plants falling over, both from the weight of the flower head and from the effects of strong winds, especially when the tubs or vases are standing on verandahs or other exposed places.

Above *Planting hyacinths. Work bulb fibre evenly around the bulbs. Do not make it too firm or roots will force up the bulbs.*

Above *Bring bulb fibre to 13 mm (½ in) below rim, leaving tops of bulbs just exposed.*
Below *Crocus chrysanthus. Good for pots.*

Agapanthus umbellatus. Flower spikes are produced in succession throughout summer.

Containers

With such a wide range of lovely species and varieties of bulbous subjects available, it is not always easy to decide what to grow. Consideration should be given to the receptacles to be used, the surroundings, exposure to weather, and the hardiness or otherwise of the bulbs chosen. Window boxes, tubs, hanging baskets, vases and all manner of containers can be used. Most will take up little space, but when filled with bulbs they give freshness, colour and gaiety both in prominent positions and in corners that would otherwise be dull and uninteresting.

For good results, window boxes ought to be not less than 18 to 20cm (7 to 8in) deep. If they are any shallower they will be inclined to dry out quickly. Stone and concrete boxes are sometimes 'built in' on new buildings, while metal boxes, made from an assortment of building materials, can be bought. The attractive terracotta pottery boxes are, unfortunately, rarely to be obtained. Some gardeners like to paint or decorate the front of outdoor window boxes but do not try anything gaudy or out of keeping with the rest of the house.

When planting window boxes it is important not to use a lot of different varieties for all will not flower at the same time. For the spring, daffodils, hyacinths and early tulips are available in many colours. Smaller bulbs can be planted along the front, *Scilla sibirica*, *Muscari armeniacum* and crocus can be used, although there is sometimes a problem with sparrows picking out the centres of the yellow crocuses. Strands of black cotton or small twigs placed round the plants keep sparrows off but are unsightly. Try placing a saucer of water nearby as often the birds are seeking moisture. When choosing bulbs to be grown near the house, pay regard to the colour of the walls. For white or cement-washed walls, yellow, orange and red will stand out; against red bricks, white, lilac and mauve look well.

Boxes or vases of any kind can be treated with cuprinol or another non-toxic agent. After this preservative has dried, apply one or two coats of a good stain or paint but never use creosote which is poisonous to plants. Hanging baskets can often be situated in positions where it is impossible to place any other type of container. They vary greatly in size, construction and material, although more are made of wire or metal than of wood. It is essential to line all baskets with moss, etc., not only to prevent the compost falling out, but in order to retain moisture. Window boxes suspended over pathways should be made with a removable basal tray so that drainage water is collected and can be easily removed. An inverted saucer or plate at the bottom of a hanging basket will ensure that drainage is good and that the compost does not become too wet through overwatering.

Early hyacinths and some narcissi, such as Paper White and Grand Soleil d'Or, can be grown in bowls of pebbles. Bulbs grown in pebbles or shingle should be placed in the pebbles, but their base should be kept just above the water which collects at the bottom of the bowl. Keep pebbles moist but not waterlogged. Growing hyacinths in water is another old-fashioned way of obtaining early colour; it is best to use the special narrow glass vases, cup-shaped at the top where the bulbs are placed, with a shaped neck to prevent the bulbs falling to the bottom. They are made in plain or tinted glass, but specially beautiful, coloured specimens are also available. The glasses are filled with water until it almost touches the base of the bulbs. A lump of charcoal will keep the water sweet. Kept in a cool place, roots will soon develop. Top up with water as necessary and turn the glasses periodically to prevent irregular growth. It is possible to obtain little holders which clasp the bulb in the cup of the hyacinth glass and so prevent it from falling over. Bulbs grown in water often become hollow and therefore useless for the following year. Those that remain firm should be planted in the garden.

Choosing the bulbs

There is such a wide range of suitable bulbs for growing in bowls and pots that it is not easy to make a choice. Some, of course, have been grown in containers for many years and may be relied upon to give good results. The aim of many gardeners is to have bulbs in bloom by Christmas. This is certainly possible provided the right varieties are grown.

There are a few varieties of daffodils and tulips and well over a dozen varieties of specially-prepared hyacinths available for Christmas-flowering. These special bulbs of hyacinths and tulips must be planted before the middle of September and brought into warmth in the first week of December. Christmas-flowering daffodils should be planted during the first week in October and taken into the living room at the very beginning of December.

In addition to these prepared bulbs, hyacinths which are easy to force include the early-flowering Anna Maria, pink; Bismarck, porcelain blue; Delft Blue, light blue; L'Innocence, white; Jan Bos, crimson-red; Lady Derby, shell pink; and Ostara, dark blue. These are followed by Amethyst, lilac-violet; Blue Jacket, dark blue; Carnegie, pure white; and City of Haarlem, yellow.

Next come the following narcissi:

Poetaz or bunch-flowered narcissus: Cragford, white orange cup; Geranium, similar to, but larger than, Cragford; Laurens Koster, white, yellow cup.

Small-cupped narcissus: Barrett Browning, white, red cup; Birma, yellow, orange-scarlet cup; and Verger, white, deep red cup.

Large-cupped narcissus: Carlton, soft yellow; Flower Record, white, yellow cup, edged orange; Ice Follies, pure white.

Double narcissus: Cheerfulness, several creamy yellow flowers on a stem; Van Sion, golden yellow.

Narcissus triandrus, pure white flowers in clusters.

Narcissus cyclamineus: February Gold, yellow; Peeping Tom, rich golden yellow.

Among the many trumpet varieties, usually referred to as daffodils, the following can be forced or grown in the living room under cooler conditions:

Yellow trumpet: Dutch Master, Golden Harvest.

White trumpet: Mount Hood and the smaller W. P. Milner.

Bicolor trumpet: Magnet, white petals, yellow trumpet.

There are also a number of excellent dwarf narcissi which respond well to bowl and pot culture. Among the best are N. bulbocodium conspicuus, golden yellow; N. minimus, yellow; Nanus, yellow; and N. triandrus albus, often known as Angel's Tears, creamy white.

Tulips are also widely grown in bowls and again the range of varieties is very wide. Among the best of the single earlies are Bellona, golden yellow; General de Wet, fiery orange, stippled scarlet; Prince of Austria, rich orange-red, sweetly scented; Couleur Cardinal, purplish crimson; and Christmas Marvel, cherry pink, all about 38 cm (15 in) tall. The double early varieties grow 25 to 30 cm (10 to 12 in) high and include Electra, cherry red; Maréchal Niel, yellow and orange; Peach Blossom, rosy pink; Murillo, blush pink; and Vuurbaak, bright scarlet.

The Triumph and Mendel sections also grow well in bowls and they, too, are available in very many colours. Particularly good are Mendel Apricot Beauty, which is salmon-rose and Golden Olga, red, edged yellow,

both growing 40 cm (16 in) and flowering in January. Slightly taller are the Triumph varieties: Attila, purple-violet and Kees Nelis, red, edged yellow, flowering mid-February.

Most of the Darwin varieties, which flower a little later, are too tall for bowl and pot culture, although they look well in larger containers. Some of the tulip species are also attractive when grown in bowls: they include *T. clusiana*, cherry red and white; and *T. kaufmanniana*, yellowish white, carmine band.

With the smaller bulbs there is a remarkable variety suitable for pot and bowl culture.

Achimenes are specially attractive.

Start them indoors in February using the trays, boxes or pots in which they are to flower. Any peaty, sandy mixture is suitable. Grow in good compost and apply liquid feed when in full growth. Pinch out shoots to induce bushy growth. Separate colours are available but a mixture of mauve, blue, pink, red and white funnel or tubular flowers throughout summer always look attractive. Dry off the tubers in autumn and store in a frost proof place.

Begonia pendula is often known as the basket begonia because of its suitability for boxes and baskets. Its graceful trailing stems are furnished with smallish pointed leaves and an

abundance of small pendulous flowers which, with the foliage, will often hide the containers in which they are growing. The tubers should be planted in February or March. Avoid overfeeding, otherwise ungainly growth and fewer flowers are likely. Named varieties and separate colours are available.

Begonia multiflora in single or double forms and many colours can be treated in the same way, although growth is more upright. These begonias will usually continue flowering until late September, when they should be dried off and stored.

Ornamental ivy and begonias in a window box.

Bulbs do not suffer from being grown in a container. Provided the soil mixture is good, there is no reason why they should not be grown for two or three years in the same pot or box. However, most can be planted out in the garden after one year in a container, so that a fresh

supply of bulbs can be planted in the containers each year.

Chionodoxa sardensis, porcelain-blue and *C. luciliae*, bright blue, white in the centre, both grow 15 cm (6 in) high

Cyclamen are understandably very popular pot plants for providing winter colour indoors.

and require little warmth. Crocus species are most attractive including *C. imperati*, violet and lilac and the *C. chrysanthus* forms such as Blue Pearl; Cream Beauty; E. P. Bowles, yellow and brown; and Snowbunting, white, feathered purple. The larger Dutch varieties include Queen of Blues, silvery lilac; Remembrance, deep purple; and Snowstorm, white. The yellow varieties, however, do not always succeed in bowls.

For late summer- and autumn-flowering, some of the large colchicums give a fine display, blooming from August onwards. They are mostly in shades of lilac, rose, mauve or white and the striking 15 cm (6 in) bulbs usually produce flowers if placed on a saucer without soil or water on a sunny shelf, but they are useless after flowering by this method.

Eranthis or winter aconites produce their rich yellow flowers surrounded by green bracts on very short stems from January onwards. They do not need warmth but prefer a gritty, humus-rich compost.

Freesias always prove attractive in pots. Their culture is described on page 31.

Fritillaria meleagris likes a peaty compost. The bulbs should be potted in October and must be kept under cool conditions. Space them about 8 cm (3 in) apart, for each 20 cm (8 in) stem will produce two or three, six pointed, squared-off, drooping bells.

Galanthus or snowdrops do not like high temperatures but the single and double forms can be potted in autumn and kept outdoors until they show signs of flower buds when they can be moved into warmth.

Gloriosa does best in good-sized, well-drained pots of fairly rich soil supplemented by feeding with liquid seaweed fertilizer when in growth. It needs warmth in summer, while in winter a temperature well above freezing point should be provided. The best known species are G. *rothschildiana* and the slightly taller G. *superba*.

Several varieties of irises are ideal for pot and bowl display. The easiest to manage is *I. reticulata*, 13 to 15 cm (5 to 6 in), velvety purple flowers with a gold splash on the lower petals, and very fragrant. It has a number of forms including Cantab, light

Sturdy, hardy, early-flowering Iris danfordiae. The bulbs divide after flowering.

blue, and J. S. Dijt, reddish purple. *I. danfordiae* has lemon yellow flowers on 8 cm (3 in) stems. Bulbs grown for flowering in the greenhouse or living room in the early part of the year should be plunged in peat, etc., in a cellar or sheltered place outdoors until they are well rooted before being taken into a temperature of 10 to 12 deg. C (50 to 55°F). Keep them moist until the foliage fades, then allow them to dry off for the summer.

Ixias are splendid for early summer flowering. The pots do not require covering after planting. Place five bulbs 13 mm (½ in) deep in a 13 cm (5 in) pot, and stand them in a sheltered place until top growth is advancing. Then move them to a cool, light position. There are separate varieties and mixtures, the 38 to 45 cm (15 to 18 in) stems bearing many coloured blooms with dark centres.

Leucocoryne ixioides odorata produces delicate sky-blue, funnel-shaped, scented flowers on 35 to 45 cm (15 to 18 in) stems. It can be grown in the same way as freesias.

Muscari or grape hyacinths are excellent indoors if not forced. Keep the pot outdoors or in the cold frame until February. *M. botryoides caeruleum* and Heavenly Blue are most reliable; *M. azureum* is dwarf-growing.

The most important feature of schizostylis is that it blooms in mid-autumn, sometimes in late November, when there is little other colour available. It is an excellent pot plant. Best known varieties are the pink Kaffir Lilies, Mrs. Hegarty and Viscountess Byng.

Of the scilla species, the Siberian Squill is popular because of its rich blue flowers. It must not be forced but should be grown under cool conditions. *S. sibirica* and its better form Spring Beauty are most reliable.

Sparaxis (the Harlequin Flower) can be grown in exactly the same way as ixias. On 30 cm (12 in) stems it produces velvety scarlet flowers with yellow and black centres.

Streptanthera cuprea coccinea is allied to sparaxis and can also be grown in the same way as ixias. It has flat, open, salver-shaped blooms up to 5 cm (2 in) across, of a vivid capsicum-red colour and a crimson and black centre.

Tecophilaea cyanocrocus is known as the Chilean Crocus. It has rich gentian-blue flowers with a white throat. It can be grown outdoors in sunny positions but is at its best as a pot plant.

Known by several names including brodiaea, ipheion and milla, tritelias are spring-flowering; they can be cultivated in the same way as crocuses but should not be forced. *T. uniflora* produces star-shaped, pale violet-blue, sweetly-scented flowers on 10 to 15 cm (4 to 6 in) stems. Its tufts of leaves are an added attraction.

Tritonia crocata should be grown in pots and can also be grown in the same way as ixias. The flowers are like those of montbretia but wider. It prefers a sandy loam. Five bulbs

should be planted in each 13 cm (5 in) pot, which if possible should be kept in a cold frame covered with peat until growth is seen. The tawny red flowers on 45 to 60 cm (18 to 24 in) stems appear in summer. Some kinds have rose-pink or red flowers.

Zephyranthes, often known as the Flower of the Western World and the Zephyr Flower, is an excellent pot plant. *Z. candida* is the best known with pure white, crocus-like flowers in September.

In addition, there are several pendulous – growing, tuberous perennials requiring a temperature of 15 to 18 deg. C (60 to 65°F).

CHAPTER 7
Bulbs for Greenhouse Display

When considering the planting of bulbs it is natural to think mainly of those that flower outdoors during spring and summer. As we have seen in Chapter One, however, there are many interesting and colourful species that will provide flowers from July until December.

If spring-flowering bulbs are grown in the greenhouse border or in pots or boxes, it is possible to raise blooms long before those outdoors are anywhere near flowering; this is so whether the greenhouse is heated or not. There is, therefore, an opportunity to cultivate some of the more exotic subjects which are not fully hardy and which may be marked or discoloured by heavy autumn rains or frosts.

'Preparing' bulbs

Commercially, millions of bulbs are forced in greenhouses each year. Fortunately many bulbs used for forcing are produced in this country but large quantities are still imported. It is essential to use good bulbs: it is a false economy to do otherwise. Aim to plant firm, plump, medium-sized, thoroughly-ripened specimens, free from damage or disease. The treatment which bulbs receive in the early stages of their life has an important effect upon their flowering, in both time and quality. This has been proved in several ways, notably in that bulbs produced in the South of France will usually flower earlier than those raised in this country or in similar locations.

As the result of scientific investigations carried out in Holland and elsewhere, it has long been known that the time between the lifting and planting of bulbs, so often referred to as the resting period, is a time of great activity inside the bulb. It was found that the bulb's environment during that time has a most important effect upon its following flowering period and the quality of the flowers produced.

Nearly eighty years ago a Dutch bulb grower, Nicolaas Dames, did invaluable work regarding the early forcing of hyacinths. He exposed them during their ripening period to conditions which would make them more suitable for early forcing. One of his notable achievements was to lift bulbs four or five weeks earlier than usual and place them in a shed or similar place where the temperature was kept for some weeks at 29 deg. C (95°F). This meant that the bulbs had to be lifted while the foliage was still green and was cut down. At that time the development of the next year's leaves inside the bulb was already beginning in the normal way. Placing the bulbs under high temperatures for ripening stops the development of new leaves and encourages flower formation. This led to the marketing of so-called 'prepared' bulbs for early forcing and there are now several methods for preparing bulbs for growing in pots and other containers. They include planting bulbs, including hyacinths and tulips, in the open ground where the soil is warmed artificially over electric cables or even in hot beds.

In greenhouses there should be no

Lilium auratum. Golden rayed Lily of Japan.

difficulty in having prepared hyacinths in flower at Christmas or even earlier. There are also a few treated daffodils available for early flowering. There are, however, many other bulbous subjects which make poor growth and are unsatisfactory if any attempt is made to prepare them, although trade growers use a method known as pre-cooling daffodils which gives good results. It·involves keeping bulbs at a temperature of 9 deg. C (48°F) for seven or eight weeks and then moving them to different temperatures.

Check the bulbs

When growing bulbs, whether in the greenhouse or in the garden, unpack them as soon as they arrive from the supplier; this is frequently indicated on the bag. Not only does such action give the opportunity to check on the right variety and quantity, but if bulbs are left packed for any length of time they soon become soft and begin to decay. Never plant damaged or soft bulbs. Always check that the basal plate is sound and firm. Never leave the bulbs heaped one upon another. If they cannot be planted at once, place them in a cool, aerated place.

Which bulbs?

There is a very large range of delightful bulbous plants that are very easy to grow in the greenhouse and that do not require any special culture either before or after planting. They require more congenial conditions than alpine house or living room subjects, which will withstand irregular temperatures and indifferent treatment. Bulbs in containers in the greenhouse can be left for several years, with some additional feeding.

Achimenes

Most of these tuberous perennials are natives of Central and South America. Closely related to gloxinias, they are first class for hanging baskets in a cool greenhouse, or for warm outdoor positions in summer. There are two types, those that cascade in baskets or over the edge of the greenhouse staging and the upright types which require a few sticks for sup-

port. They like well-drained, porous compost containing peat, leaf mould or compost heap matter. The rhizomes are small, some resembling tiny catkins, others looking like dried peas. They should be started into growth from February to April and kept in a temperature around 15 deg. C (60°F). Once growth is seen, the plants should be placed in full light and the temperature can be reduced gradually to 12 deg. C (55°F). Allow three plants to a 13cm (5in) pot, and up to a dozen in hanging baskets. They flower from June onwards according to planting time. The colour range is very wide. Known as 'hot water plants', they can be given water with the chill off but not hot.

Agapanthus

Sometimes known as African Lilies or Love Flowers, these plants have somewhat short rhizomes with thick fleshy roots, strap-shaped leaves and stems bearing funnel-shaped flowers. They are best grown in pots or

tubs in the conservatory or cool greenhouse although in mild districts they thrive in sunny positions in sandy loam and leaf mould.

A. umbellatus is the best known species, producing stout flower stems 60 to 90cm (2 to 3ft) high, bearing umbels of bright blue flowers. It has both a double and a white form. *A. caulescens* is similar, as is *A. mooreanus*, while the *A. ardernei* hybrids take in many fine shades of blue. Propagation is by division in spring; seed is rarely available.

Babiana (see also page 26)

First class for growing in pots in a cool greenhouse. Six bulbs in a 13cm (5in) pot will, if planted in October, give a superb display in May and June. They are usually offered in mixture but *B. stricta* is a strain producing flowers of creamy yellow, lilac, blue or crimson, on 25 to 30cm (10 to 12in) stems.

Babianas like a sunny position.

Begonia

This is a very large family of plants with a widely different habit of growth. There are hundreds of the tuberous species and varieties in cultivation. It is possible to raise many from seeds but the easiest method is to plant the dry tubers which can be started into growth in warmth from January until April. Started in March, they will require little heat and begin to produce flowers from mid-July onwards. A temperature in the range 10 to 18 deg. C (50 to 65°F) but not higher, should be provided. Plump, firm tubers should be used. These can be placed in small pots or shallow boxes containing a good layer of peat or leaf mould covered with a mixture of peaty, sandy loam. The plants in boxes can be potted singly when they are growing well. The tubers should be barely covered, although many gardeners prefer to leave the tops exposed to avoid moisture settling there. A fairly moist, buoyant temperature encourages good growth, and plants can be given larger pots according to growth. They are first class for greenhouse and living room decoration. For planting outdoors for summer bedding, the tubers need not be boxed until April, for they should not be planted in the open ground until early June.

There are single and double varieties in a wide colour range, both in named sorts and mixtures. Apart from the large flowering varieties, there is a section known as *B. multiflora*, having fairly small but freely produced flowers, while the pendula or basket varieties, both single and double, are excellent for hanging baskets and window boxes. All should be dried and stored in a frost proof place in winter.

Calochortus

Sometimes known as Butterfly Tulips, or Mariposa Lilies, these are charming for the cold greenhouse. If eight or nine bulbs are planted in a 13 cm (5 in) pot of sandy, peaty loam in November and kept in the cold frame to root until late December,

they will give a cheerful display in summer. There are several varieties and mixtures with stems of 30 to 38 cm (12 to 15 in).

Cyclamen persicum (see also page 29)

This is one of the most popular of winter-flowering pot plants. Tubers are usually available from early August onwards and should be potted up in August placing one in each 13 cm (5 in) pot of fresh sandy loam, to which leaf mould or peat has been added. Leave the top of the tuber just exposed so that water cannot settle there. Grow in a temperature of 15 to 18 deg. C (60 to 65°F). Water carefully giving liquid feeds as the first flower buds unfold, making sure that the liquid does not settle on the tubers. Gradually dry off the tubers in spring for starting into growth again in August. A wide colour range is available and there are now strains in which the flowers are scented; in others the petals are fringed or crimped. *Cycla-*

men persicum can also be raised in mixture from seed sown in early autumn or in February when a temperature around 15 deg. C (60°F) is required.

Daffodil (see Narcissus)

Eucharis

These warm greenhouse plants of great beauty and delightful fragrance bloom in winter and spring. They flourish in a moist, minimum summer temperature of 18 deg. C (65°F) and during their winter rest need around 13 deg. C (55°F). When in growth they require plenty of water and liquid feeds. *E. grandiflora* has stems up to 60 cm (2 ft) high with pure white, strongly scented, glistening bells. The roundish bulbs are 13 to 18 cm (5 to 7 in) in diameter. The white flowers of *E. candida* are flushed yellow. Repot after the flowering period is over using rich loamy soil or John Innes No. 3 compost.

Calochortus superbus. *Of unusual shape, the Butterfly Tulips have a wide colour range.*

Eucomis comosa (punctata)

This is a South African plant of which the yellowish green, shaded purple flowers in summer are closely formed on stems usually about 45 cm (18 in) high. Single bulbs should be grown in 13 cm (5 in) pots or three can be placed in the 17 cm (7 in) size. They like plentiful supplies of water during spring and summer, reducing in autumn so that the roots are dry by winter when a temperature of 7 deg. C (45°F) is sufficient.

The shorter growing species include E. autumnalis (undulata), greenish yellow; E. bicolor, whitish edged purple, 30 cm (1 ft) high. Rarely seen is the tall growing, 1.50 m (5 ft) high, E. pole-evansii, with yellowish green florets.

Freesia (see also page 31)

Their graceful appearance and scent, combined with a very wide colour range and long flowering season, have made freesias one of the most desirable of bulbous plants. On stems often branched up to 60 cm (2 ft) high, the irregular, funnel shaped flowers open in succession.

The present day varieties are derived chiefly from F. refracta which has strongly scented, creamy yellow funnel shaped flowers. The strongest perfume is still to be found in the creamy yellow or orange varieties, but the modern lavender-blue, blue-mauve and red varieties are extremely attractive. The earliest freesia flowers come from seed raised plants. Sowings can be made from April onwards in pots or boxes, five or six seeds to a 13 cm (5 in) pot of John Innes No. 1 compost. They germinate best in a temperature of 18 deg. C (65°F) and flowers should appear from September.

Gladiolus (see also page 32)

The majority of this large family are most suited to outdoor culture, but the early flowering Nanus group varieties are splendid when grown in pots in a cool greenhouse. They should be planted in October, five corms in a 15 cm (6 in) pot of good, well-drained compost. Place the pots in a sheltered place outdoors or in a cold frame so that a good root system develops. Bring them into the greenhouse in December; they should flower from early April onwards. These Nanus varieties grow about 60 cm (2 ft) high. Dainty cultivars, ideal for cutting, include Amanda Mahy, orange-scarlet; Blushing Bride, white, carmine flaking; Peach Blossom, shell pink; and The Bride, pure white, early flowering.

Gloxinia speciosa

This name is likely to be in continuing use although in its correct title of the plant is Sinningia speciosa. Cultivation is generally the same as for tuberous begonias, the tubers being planted in February or March in pots, with their tops barely covered with fairly rich, peaty compost. A temperature of 18 deg. C (65°F) is suitable. Move the plants to bigger pots as growth proceeds and water as necessary with occasional liquid feeds; avoid wetting the foliage.

Propagation is by stem and leaf cuttings, but seed forms an easy means of obtaining a stock. Sow from December onwards in a temperature of 18 to 20 deg. C (65 to 70°F) and water carefully. Flowering plants can be obtained within six months of sowing. Seeds and tubers are usually offered in mixtures although it is possible to obtain separate varieties or colours.

Eucomis punctata. Known as the Pineapple Flower because of its clustered flower spike.

Haemanthus

This family of African plants has the common names of 'blood flower' and 'shaving brush'. Excellent for the cool greenhouse, they make a good show when grown in large pots or tubs. The flowers, produced in umbels, have long petals and long prominent stamens, the coloured bracts increasing the show.

Once potted, leave the bulbs undisturbed as long as possible. Plant so that the neck of the bulb is just below the surface.

H. albiflos has white or greenish flowers on 30 cm (1 ft) stems during the summer. H. coccineus produces coral red flowers in September on 23 cm (9 in) stems and before the leaves appear. H. katherinae shows its bright scarlet flowers on 30 to 60 cm (1 to 2 ft) stems during July and August.

Hippeastrum

These popular pot plants are sometimes referred to as Amaryllis from which they are botanically quite separate. They produce large red, trumpet-shaped flowers, usually four at a time on a sturdy stem 60 cm (2 ft) high. Pink and white forms are also available.

The large bulbs should be potted as soon as they are received. Use clean 13 to 17 cm (5 to 7 in) pots, one bulb per pot, according to size. Hippeastrums like well-drained soil, fairly rich in organic matter. John Innes Potting Compost No. 3 is ideal or a home made potting mixture can be prepared of three parts good loam and one part well-decayed manure together with some silver sand and bone meal.

Ensure good drainage by placing some broken crocks at the bottom of the pot and cover these with a thin hybrids are usually sold by colour rather than by named varieties.

Hyacinth (see also page 34)

Hyacinths make a good display in pots in the greenhouse. They can be planted from August onwards using a peaty loam instead of bulb fibre mixture.

Hymenocallis

Sometimes known as Sea Daffodils, these are excellent for greenhouse cultivation. The bulbs should be potted in March in a mixture of loam, old manure and silver sand. Keep the pots in a temperature of 18 deg. C (65°F) and water as necessary. They need repotting only once in three years. After they have flowered in summer, water should be gradually withheld so that the bulbs can have a short rest.

H. amancaes has bright yellow, spreading flowers on 45 cm (18 in) stems. It can be grown outdoors in summer but must be taken indoors and kept dry in winter. *H. narcissiflora (calathina)* bears fragrant white flowers in summer. It has several forms with creamy yellow or green marked flowers. Some of the hymenocallis have at various times been included with the pancratiums.

Iris (see also page 34)

For greenhouse culture there are several types suitable for pots. Any good, well-drained compost is appropriate and cool conditions are best giving a long flowering period and better colouring. *I. tingitana* potted in September will flower at Christmas. Keep them cool until November, then provide a temperature around 15 deg. C (60°F). Spanish and Dutch varieties also do well in pots. The dwarf varieties such as *I. reticulata*, velvety blue-purple, blotched orange, and *I. danfordiae*, lemon coloured, are particularly good.

Lachenalia

Known as the Cape Cowslip, this is a pleasing subject for a cool greenhouse. The bulbs should be potted in August or September, placing five in each 13 cm (5 in) pot of fairly rich

Lachenalia tricolor, *the Cape Cowslip. Produces spikes of long lasting flowers when grown in pots in the greenhouse.*

layer of oak or beech leaves to prevent the soil being washed through. Firm the soil around the bulb to a depth of 25 mm (1in) below the pot rim, leaving the top third of the bulb exposed. After potting, moisten the soil (but not the bulb) with tepid water and do not water again for ten days until new roots form and growth begins. Keep the bulbs in a day temperature round 20 deg. C (65 to 70°F).

The first sign of growth is the development of the flower head and stem slightly to the side of the centre from which the foliage subsequently emerges. Sometimes, however, the leaves develop at the same time as the flower head and may even pre-

cede it. When flowering is finished, cut out the stalk with a sharp knife 25 to 50 mm (1 to 2 in) above the bulb, but allow the foliage to develop. When no more leaves appear the bulbs have finished growing for the year, but continue to water the pot until the tips of the leaves begin to discolour. When this happens place the bulbs in a cool, dry place and allow the foliage to die down. Keep the bulbs in pots throughout the summer and autumn to enable them to rest.

From December bring the bulbs back into the warmth again, give them some tepid water, and start them into growth once more. Either add fresh potting compost or completely repot at this stage. It is not necessary to repot every year; every third year is sufficient. Hippeastrum

compost. Keep them in the cold frame until early November, then transfer to the greenhouse taking care not to overwater but giving occasional feeds of liquid manure. The flowers will appear from late January onwards. The foliage is fleshy and the 25 to 30 cm (10 to 12 in) spikes carry drooping tubular flowers from January onwards. Best known is *L. aloides* or *tricolor*, the flowers being green, banded red and yellow. Of the hybrids available, Aurea is yellow; Nelsonii, yellow, tinged green; and Quadricolor, green and orange with reddish and purplish markings.

Leucocoryne

A native of Chile, this subject, often known as Glory of the Sun, can be grown in the same way as ixias and freesias, being potted in September or October. Keep the pots in the cold frame or other sheltered position and give water as necessary. Before frosts come, move the pots to the cool greenhouse. The only species in cultivation is *L. ixioides*, producing scented, pale blue flowers on 38 to 45 cm (15 to 18 in) stems. The form known as *odorata*, flowering in March and April, has a stronger perfume.

Lilium (see also page 36)

There is no reason why lilies should not be enjoyed in the greenhouse. Always pot the bulbs as soon as obtained, first removing dead or broken scales, before dusting with yellow sulphur powder. Never use over-large pots. Provide good drainage and a porous compost. For stem rooting varieties use pots about 23 cm (9 in) deep, half-filled with compost at first, so that the bulb is covered with 10 to 13 cm (4 to 5 in). Add more compost when the stem roots develop.

Good species for pots include the following: *L. auratum*, the golden rayed Lily of Japan; *L. brownii*; *L. formosanum*; *L. hansonii*; *L. longiflorum*, the white Easter Lily; *L. regale* and *L. speciosum* and its forms; *L. tenuifolium*.

Narcissus (see also page 38)

This includes the short-cupped and crowned varieties as well as the trumpet varieties usually known as daffodils. They look best in 15 cm (6 in) pots, although for very large trumpet varieties the 20 cm (8 in) size is preferred. Use a good loamy mixture; pot firmly from August onwards, according to variety. Plunge the planted pots in weathered ashes or peat so that they root well. Once the roots have established themselves, the pots should be taken in relays to the greenhouse at about 14 day intervals. Many varieties are available as can be seen from catalogues; they include all the varieties detailed in Chapter Six as being suitable for bowl culture.

Nerine (see also page 40)

Most varieties produce their strap shaped leaves after the flowers appear. Bulbs should be potted from early July onwards placing two or three in a 13 or 15 cm (5 or 6 in) pot of rich, loamy soil. As soon as growth is seen, water freely, continuing to do so until well into the spring. From early May to July allow the bulbs to rest placing them on a shelf in the sun to bake and ripen. Repotting is necessary once every three or four years. There are various species and many named varieties including *N. flexuosa*, pink; *N. sarniensis*, the Guernsey Lily, salmon-scarlet, which has many cultivars; and *N. undulata*, rose pink.

Pancratium

Sometimes known as Sea Daffodils or Mediterranean Lilies, they can be grown outdoors in very warm, sheltered positions but are best cultivated in pots. The large bulbs produce strap shaped leaves and umbels of white scented flowers. *P. illyricum*, 45 cm (18 in), flowers in May and June and *P. maritimum* from July to September.

Polianthes tuberosa

This easily grown bulb flourishes in pots of well-drained loam enriched by rotted manure, peat and silver

Nerines are dainty plants, the flowers of which glisten in sunshine. Nerine sarniensis, the Guernsey Lily, flowers in the autumn.

sand. It can be planted from February to May to secure a succession of its highly scented blooms. Plant under warm conditions and when a good root system has been formed, move to a temperature of 15 deg. C (60°F). The white, funnel shaped flowers develop on 75 cm (2½ft) stems. The form known as 'The Pearl' is well known, growing 45 cm (18in) high; it is very sweetly scented, the leaves being marked brownish red.

Sauromatum guttatum

Frequently known as The Monarch of the East, or the Voodoo Lily, these tuberous rooted plants grow easily in pots in a greenhouse or, as a curiosity, they can be placed in a bowl or saucer in the living room without soil or water. The bulbs cannot be used again after this method. They grow rapidly producing arum-like flowers from 30 to 45 cm (1 to 1½ft) high. These are oddly speckled and marked with purple, yellow and green. After flowering in spring, the tubers should be kept in a cool place and be started again in October.

Sprekelia formosissima

This native of Mexico is the only species in the family. It has the common names of Jacobean Lily and Aztec Lily. The long-necked bulbs are excellent when grown in pots of fairly rich compost and are treated the same as hippeastrum (page 62). Outdoors, plant them 10 to 12 cm (4 to 5in) deep in good, well-drained soil in a sheltered, sunny position. Each bulb produces one or two stems usually bearing two gorgeous orchid-like red flowers in June, sometimes before the foliage appears. The bulbs must be lifted in autumn.

Streptanthera

Related to the ixia and sparaxis and requiring similar treatment, this is a charming subject for greenhouse culture in pots. S. cuprea, 23 cm (9in) high, has coppery yellow flowers marked with a black band. A form known as coccinea is intense scarlet, also banded black. Bulbs can be planted outdoors in autumn choosing a warm, sheltered, well-drained spot.

Tigridia pavonia (see also page 41)

Now available in a wide colour range, the individual flowers are short lived. Bulbs should be potted in autumn, three to a 13 cm (5 in) pot. Plunge them in peat or old ashes in the cold frame to provide good protection from frost; or, preferably, take them into the greenhouse in late October.

Tulip (see also page 42)

Tulips are easily grown in the greenhouse border and in pots or boxes. For earliest flowers, plant at the beginning of September, keeping them outdoors to form roots until November when they should be removed to the warm greenhouse. Any sweet, well-drained soil is suitable. Four bulbs in a 13 cm (5 in) pot will give a good display. The early single, early double, Mendel and Triumph groups grow well in the greenhouse as do some of the shorter growing Darwin varieties. It is also possible to obtain prepared varieties which will flower in time for Christmas.

Vallotta speciosa

This is often known as the Scarborough Lily. Of South African origin, it is an excellent plant for a cool greenhouse and has long been grown on outdoor window sills where it remains evergreen. A simple sandy compost is suitable and when in growth the roots must be liberally supplied with moisture. Bulbs are best planted or repotted in July, and left undisturbed for three years or so. *V. speciosa* itself is scarlet and is often listed as *V. purpurea*. A form known as *elata* has smaller, cherry red flowers.

Veltheimia

Useful plants for flowering in a cool greenhouse in the winter, the bulbs should be planted in early September and allowed to dry off after the leaves have died down. Use a good loamy

compost containing peat or leaf mould, silver sand and rotted manure. After two or three years, the bulbs may be divided or stock can be increased by sowing seed in trays of light soil. *V. capensis* (or *viridifolia*) has, in March, fleshy 38 to 45 cm (15 to 18 in) stems bearing tubular pinkish red, mottled green flowers. *V. deasii*, 25 to 30 cm (10 to 12 in) high, is pale pink, while *V. glauca*, 38 cm (15 in) has whitish flowers with purplish crimson markings. The leaves of all species have wavy edges.

Zantedeschia (see also page 43)

Commonly known as the Arum Lily, these tubers are suitable for growing in the greenhouse border. Work in bone meal at the rate of 56 g (2 oz) per sq m (sq yd). They can also be grown

in pots, where three tubers per pot will make an effective display. Water only when necessary and give them ventilation whenever possible.

Zephyranthes

Often known as the Flower of the Western Wind and the Zephyr Flower, these bulbs grow well in sandy, well-drained soil in a sunny position. They produce narrow, strap-shaped leaves sometimes before the flowers appear. They make excellent pot plants for a cool greenhouse and can be grown outdoors in warm sheltered positions. *Z. candida* is the best known, the pure white crocus-like flowers appearing on 15 to 20 cm (6 to 8 in) stems. *Z. grandiflora*, 30 cm (12 in), is rosy pink and *Z. rosea*, 25 to 30 cm (10 to 12 in), pale rose pink. All flower in September.

Left Tigridia pavonia. *A striking plant for sunny positions.* **Right** Zantedeschia elliottiana *flowers in early summer.*

CHAPTER 8

Propagation

There are various methods of propagating bulbous plants. The principal means are offsets, spawn, bulbils, division, scales, cuttings and seed. By far the greatest number of plants having true bulbs and corms, as well as some tuberous rooted plants, are propagated by means of offsets.

It also shows why some bulbous plants, which have previously flowered well for some years, miss a season of colour for the 'mother' bulb has divided into several sections which are not big enough to bloom for a year or two. Offsets are particularly valuable where bulbs produce little or no seeds; in such cases it would take some years to secure a supply of new plants and there is no certainty that seed raised plants remain exactly true to type.

Propagation by offsets is the easiest and quickest means of increase and each offset has the makings of a new, complete and independent flowering plant. Offsets are usually found closely attached to the parent but in a few cases, notably montbretias and tulips, they are sometimes produced on a thickish growth or runner. They are then known as 'droppers' for they are actually lower in the ground than the main bulb.

Offsets

The production of offsets in the first instance is evidence of the strength and vigour of the parent bulb since these new plants arise from the nourishment taken from the soil and through the air by the roots and healthy foliage of the growing plants. It is as if the food obtained and manufactured by the roots and leaves has compelled the original bulbs or corms to build extensive storehouses to hold the extra energy. This explains why after a few years some bulbs occupy much more than their allotted space.

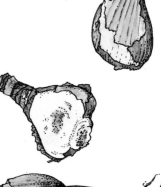

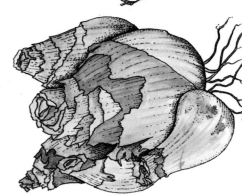

Left Where bulbs are grown and propagated on a large scale, they present an arresting display, **Below** Offsets are easily detached from the mother bulb and should be graded.

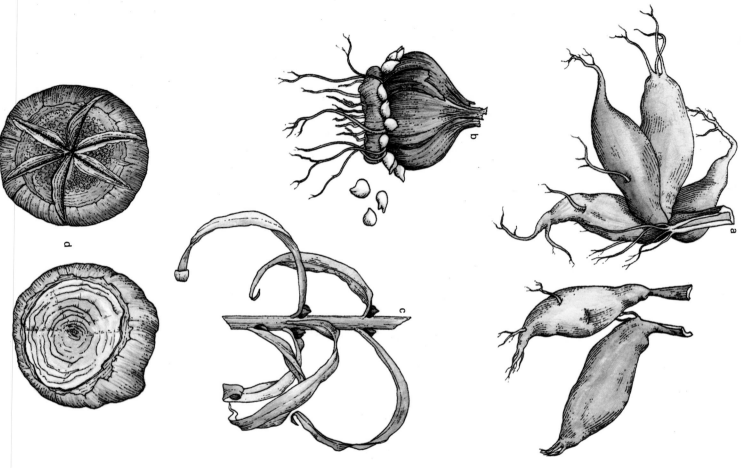

There are various methods of propagation: (a) tubers can be divided (b) gladioli make tiny cormlets (known as spawn or cloves) which can be detached (c) tulips and liliums form bulbils in the axils of aerial stems (d) cutting or scooping out the basal plate of a hyacinth will help to produce bulblets.

Offsets are best detached after the foliage has died down, although gladioli are an exception, as specialist growers usually lift these while some of the lower foliage is still green. All offsets will not be of the same size and it is wise to grade them when replanting. The best arrangement is to grow them in beds where they can be left until they become of flowering

size. Naturally the larger offsets usually flower first.

Spawn

Apart from the new corms or offsets that gladioli form, they frequently make large numbers of tiny cormlets which are popularly known as spawn (or cloves). These can be detached and stored away until the following spring, when they can be sown in drills like seed and covered with 25 mm (1 in) of lightish soil. After a couple of years they will usually have attained the size of flowering corms and are treated as such.

Bulbils

A less common means of bulb propagation, applying mostly to tulips and liliums, is by way of bulbils. These are roundish, vegetative growths, shaped more or less like a bulb and sometimes to be seen in the axils of the aerial stems. They can be removed when the foliage is dying down and subsequently planted in the normal way. These bulbils will not produce flowers as quickly as offsets but will do so much earlier than seed raised plants.

Although hyacinths will form bulblets they are slow to do so. Bulblets can, however, be induced to develop on the base of the old bulb. To do this the basal plate or disc is cut across in several places and sometimes this disc is scooped out completely. The cutting or scooping can be done a week in advance of planting. Some varieties, such as the less vigorous growing Prince Henry and La Victoire, are better suited to cross cutting than scooping.

Make sure not to cut too deeply. Two to three millimetres (1/12 in) is usually deep enough for cuts, 3 to 4 mm (1/8 in) for scooping. Scooped bulbs are often dipped in clean hydrated lime to protect the cut surfaces and to prevent them from drying out too quickly. Once the cuts have dried and callused, the bulbs can be placed in a temperature of about 20 deg. C (70°F). The mother bulb is, of course, planted with the tiny bulblets attached. These grow in the first season and can be separated from the mother when the bulbs are lifted the following autumn.

Gloxinias. These showy greenhouse and indoor plants flower freely if fed with liquid fertilizer.

Division

Division is another way of increasing a stock. In many cases this can be done in both spring and autumn, depending largely on the natural flowering time. It is done while the bulbs are dormant. It must be performed with care so that there are no ragged portions of roots which would open the way for diseases to gain a hold. Occasionally divisions can be made by pulling away offsets, cormlets or rhizomes by hand, while in other cases a sharp knife may be necessary. No protection is necessary. Tubers can be cut into two or more pieces provided that there is a growth bud as well as some stored food in each new part.

Scales

Apart from the offsets and bulbils which they produce, lilies can be propagated by scales. This can be done by carefully detaching their fleshy scales and inserting them more or less vertically into trays or pots of good sandy compost. Peat moss and silver sand are sometimes used for the rare or more difficult-to-grow varieties. Stand the planted scales in a fairly close frame or greenhouse. If neither is available, choose a warm, sheltered and semi-shaded site outdoors. After a short time a little bud is formed at the base of the scales and in due course this bud develops into a bulb. After two or three years it will have reached flow-

ering size.

With the more common and hardy lilies, the scales can be placed in drills of sandy soil in an outdoor bed where they can be left to flower. They should be moved to give them more space as they develop. Keep the soil drawn towards the scales so that they do not dry out.

Cuttings

A few tuberous rooted plants such as begonias and gloxinias can be propagated by leaf cuttings from well developed leaves. There are two ways

Two methods of propagation by leaf cutting.
(a) Make small cuts in the midribs and thick veins then lay the leaf on top of the compost making sure it is well firmed in.
(b) Simply place the stems of an upright leaf in compost making sure it is well firmed in.

to do this. The first method is to lay the leaf down flat having previously made a number of cuts in the midribs and other thicker veins. The leaf is placed on compost consisting of sand and peat moss. Some gardeners peg the leaves down to keep them in position, but this is not essential. The other method is to insert the stalk of the leaf upright, fixing the base tightly in the compost round the edge of a pot. Rooting will normally take place freely in a temperature of 15 to 18 deg. C (60 to 65°F).

Seed

While the majority of bulbous and tuberous plants can be raised by seed, there is a considerable variation in the length of time between the sowing of the seed and the development of flowering plants. A few, including begonias, cyclamens and gloxinias, can easily be brought into flower within one year, often in six to eight months; others such as narcissi, hyacinths, liliums and tulips may take five years or more to produce good, flowering-sized bulbs. Seed raised plants especially those readily fertilized by bees and other insects, are liable to vary in habit, colour and times of flowering; in some cases vigour, general constitution and hardiness can be improved. Perhaps this is what makes the matter of seed propagation so challenging, although some seed raised plants may not be worth retaining.

Seed should be sown as soon as it is ripe; but this is not always possible, especially with bought seed. Ripe seeds have deepened in colour, usually to a very dark brown, and are firm. Pans or boxes of John Innes or a similar seed compost are suitable for this purpose. Sow thinly. The depth of sowing depends on the size of the seeds which will vary according to the species being grown. For the smallest, the slightest covering of compost should be applied. For the vast majority, 6 to 7mm (¼in) is enough. A little coarse silver sand sprinkled on the surface soil after

sowing will lessen the possibility of moss or algae appearing on the surface of the containers.

The seed should be started under cool conditions. In the case of hardy subjects which have not germinated during summer or autumn, the pans can be placed outdoors to become exposed to frost, which often seems to have a stimulating effect, encouraging germination. The pots or boxes must, while outdoors, be covered with small mesh netting or something similar as a means of protection from mice, which are partial to seeds. Slugs, too, are liable to attack bulb seedlings but many safe slug baits are readily available.

Once growth is seen, the seedlings can be moved to a cool greenhouse or cold frame. In the case of hardy subjects, however, it is better to leave them outdoors to encourage bulbs to

develop rather than a lot of early top growth. Ideally, the seedlings should not be pricked out or disturbed the first season, but allowed to develop without a check; this is one good reason for sowing thinly. Keep the compost moist. Tender and half hardy subjects need sowing in a cool greenhouse or warm frame and require a little more attention than hardy subjects. They will need occasional watering but do not water too heavily or the surface of the soil may cake, thus preventing the seedlings from breaking through. Once the seedlings have emerged, watering again must be sparing to avoid 'damping off' (a fungal disease). Patience is required over these hardy subjects as up to a year may elapse before there are signs of germination and some years will pass before a flowering-size bulb has developed.

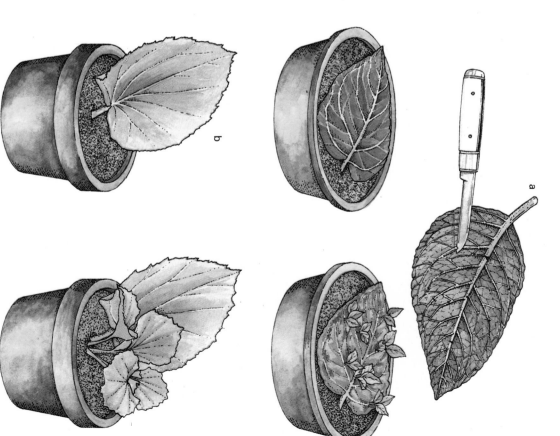

Above Cyclamen persicum are attractive winter and spring-flowering greenhouse and living room subject. A cold greenhouse or cold frame will encourage flower buds.

Below On the left is the female parent, its stamens have been removed. Pollen is transferred to its stigma from the stamens of the male bloom using a fine brush.

Hybridization

Many subjects hybridize themselves. This explains why in established colonies of bulbs or corms several different shades of colour may be found, while there may also be some variation in the pattern of growth. It is, of course, possible for the amateur gardener to do a certain amount of hybridizing. This does, however, require patience. The flower chosen for the female parent has its stamens removed, so that the pollen does not mature and this prevents self-pollination. The pollen from the selected male bloom is then transferred to the stigma of the female flower by means of a very fine-haired brush. Then it is a matter of waiting. Outdoors the pollinated flowers can be covered with a bag to give protection until the seed has set. In due course the ripened seed is collected, dried and then sown in the normal way.

CHAPTER 9

Pests and Disorders

In clean, well-managed gardens and surroundings there should be little to fear from pests and diseases especially if they are dealt with immediately they are seen or suspected. Often disorders come from plants growing nearby and it becomes necessary to destroy such sources. It is easy to become discouraged when plants die for no apparent reason, but investigation will usually show what has happened.

Even so, conditions sometimes arise for which one cannot immediately find a cause. It is, therefore, an advantage to be able to recognize any signs in their early stages, so that the correct action can be taken.

particular. The brown spots on the leaves turn grey and spread and, if not treated, the leaves and sometimes the stem also will collapse, weakening the plant for the next season. All growing and fallen leaves should be burned. *B. tulipae* has the common name of 'tulip fire' and tulip mould. The stunted plants wither, showing distinct greyish areas on both leaves and flowers. If one or two specimens are affected they can be lifted and burned. This also applies

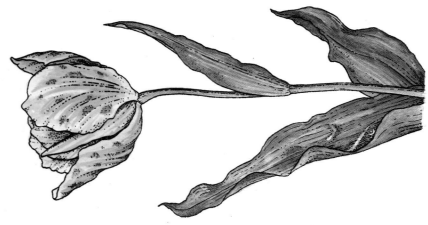

Botrytis

There are various forms of botrytis that attack bulbs. Of fungus origin, they are most destructive in a wet season or in other damp conditions. The spores often settle on the soft growth of plants with tender foliage. The symptoms are spotted and mottled areas on leaves and stems. The disease can usually be checked if dealt with at the earliest stages by spraying with a copper fungicide such as Bordeaux mixture. All forms of botrytis tend to spread quickly so carry on spraying throughout the growing season.

A form of botrytis known as *B. elliptica* attacks *Lilium candidum* in

Left *Well-cared for bulbs will produce magnificent flowers like these parrot tulips with prettily serrated petal edges.* **Right** *Tulip fire must be dealt with immediately.*

to the bulbs if at lifting time brownish lesions are seen underneath the outer skin. Any clean, healthy bulbs can be sprayed with a fungicide such as Tulisan.

Smoulder (Fire) disease

Smoulder or Fire disease can be destructive to the narcissus and research workers are still trying to find out more about the life cycle of this fungus. Large numbers of disease spores are produced. Sometimes the flowers develop normally but where the infection is severe they remain small and short stemmed. Because the fungus appears on one side of the leaves, they twist and fall to the ground showing a yellowish brown discoloration. Lift suspected bulbs. If affected bulbs are cut lengthwise, they will show brownish black stains between the scales. Infected plants should be burnt and narcissus should not be planted in the same soil again for five or more years.

The same treatment should be given to narcissus bulbs found to be rotten on being lifted. This is usually due to grey bulb rot which is a form of sclerotinia (see below).

Gladiolus disorders

Gladioli are subject to several fungal diseases. These include dry rot, the first signs of which are sometimes seen after growth has been developing for some weeks. The leaves discolour from the top downwards, eventually becoming brown and dry. As the new developing corms usually become infected, too, the entire plant should be destroyed.

Neck rot disease first shows itself by small reddish spots on the foliage. As they become larger and spread, the top growth topples over and a clear gum-like substance is emitted at the point where the leaf stem breaks. Some gardeners dip all corms in a calomel solution before planting. Mix the calomel with water to make a thin paste.

Hard rot produces purplish brown spots on the leaves; growth becomes stunted and flowering is prevented. This appears to be a soil borne disease, most likely during wet seasons. Avoid growing gladioli on the same site for some years.

Botrytis rot attacks the corms. It is seen as a greying mould leading to decay in the centre of the corm, producing the condition usually known as core rot. Destroy affected corms and choose new sites for the following season.

Fusarium yellow is a disease attacking the roots of the gladiolus leading to the yellowing of the foliage. Clean growing conditions help to avoid this disorder and affected corms should not be allowed to touch healthy specimens.

Gladioli can suffer from a variety of fungal diseases. Take immediate action as soon as any of the tell-tale signs are seen.

neck rot

dry rot

hard rot

fusarium yellow

botrytis rot

fusarium yellow

Hyacinth disorders

Hyacinths are sometimes affected by 'yellow disease', seen in its earliest stages as yellow spots on the exterior. If squeezed these exude a yellow liquid, thus spreading the bacteria causing the trouble. To escape this disease care should be taken to avoid bruising or otherwise damaging bulbs at lifting or planting time. It is best to destroy any bulbs which have yellow disease.

Loose bud is another hyacinth disorder in which the flower stem ceases to grow after it is 5 to 7.5 cm (2 to 3 in) high. The cause is unknown: it may be due to greatly varying temperatures or to the gripping of the neck of the bulb when planting. Bulbs should be held round the base or wider part. Sometimes hyacinths fail to make any roots and produce only very little top growth. Again the cause is unknown; it could arise from the bulbs being lifted in an unripe condition or exposed to high temperatures so guard against these situations when moving the bulbs.

Ink Spot

The bulbous iris, particularly the *reticulata* group, is sometimes affected by a disorder known as Ink Spot or Ink Disease. It is seen as black patches over the outer tunic of the bulb and gradually spreads until the whole bulb decays and falls apart. No suspected bulb should be planted or stored. There is as yet no effective remedy.

Sclerotinia

The tall growing *Fritillaria imperialis* is sometimes attacked by sclerotinia fungus. The symptoms are a yellowing of the foliage and a falling away of the flower stem, the bulbs deteriorating into a nasty black mess. If diseased bulbs are not taken up and destroyed, the spores left in the soil will increase to infect more bulbs the following year.

Shanking

Shanking is a disease which may appear in forced tulips. The flower buds shrivel and the leaves gradually decay. It appears to be a soil borne disorder and where the trouble has occurred the previous year, the pots or boxes should be watered with a dilution of formalin, one part to forty nine parts of water.

Bacteria

There are a number of bacteria that spoil bulbous plants. They spread by various means including rain, wind and human beings, causing leaf spottings and sometimes affecting bulbs and tubers. Many have little perma-

If seen, the rare lily beetle should be reported to the district horticultural officer.

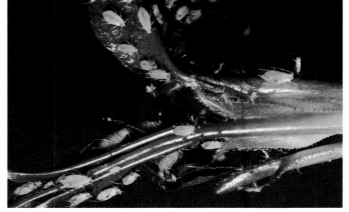

Small bulb fly larvae or grubs cause spongy decay. Burn the affected bulb.

Aphids, most common of pests. Spray or dust with derris at first signs of activity.

Vine weevil larvae feed on corms and tubers, particularly cyclamen and begonias.

nent effect. If suspected, plants should be sprayed several times with a fungicide, but any rotting bulbs must be destroyed.

Pests – generally

Every effort should be made to detect the presence of pests at the earliest possible moment; they must be destroyed before they increase in number. Every part of a plant above and below ground is liable to be attacked. It is therefore wise to know something of the different pests, their habits, methods of feeding and the best ways of combating them.

There are two main groups – biting and sucking. The biters are destroyed by stomach poisons through dusting or spraying, while the sucking type can be killed by systemic insecticides, contact washes or under glass, by fumigants.

There are, of course, larger animal pests that sometimes attack bulbous plants. These include mice which will spoil many bulbs including those in store: various rodent destroyers are readily available. Country gardeners in particular may find that rabbits will eat the young growths of bulbous plants including lilies. Bulbs can be surrounded by wire netting, although more drastic action may be needed if the attacks are serious.

Eelworms

Various bulbs, including hyacinths, irises, narcissi, snowdrops and tulips, are sometimes attacked by stem and bulb eelworms. They are so small that they are only visible under a microscope. Leaves becomes malformed, twisted and streaked. When affected bulbs are lifted and cut, brown rings or patches will be found in the scales, while in some subjects, including tulips, the flowers will not develop. Infected bulbs should be burnt, although the hot water treatment for narcissi (see below) lessens the possibility of fatal attacks. Where this cannot be done the bulbs must be burnt and a fresh site used the following year.

Flies

Narcissus flies can be most destructive. There are three types, one of which is much larger than the other two. This is known as the Merodon fly. This comes from a large whitish larva which burrows into the bulbs causing them to become soft and spongy. Leaves are few, weak, and distorted. All affected bulbs should be burnt. The fly lays eggs near the bulbs in the spring. Some protection can be given by dusting around the bulbs with lindane from late March to mid-June. Professional growers immerse the bulbs in water at a temperature of 44 deg. C (110°F) for one hour; this kills the grubs and does not harm the bulbs. The smaller Eumerus flies also attack other bulbs and can be treated in the same way as the larger species.

Mites

Bulb scale mites live between the scales of daffodils and narcissi causing softness and death. Immersing dormant bulbs in water at 44 deg. C (110°F) will kill the mites.

Slugs and Snails

Slugs and snails can do a great deal of harm in the bulb garden, eating the young shoots and leaves. They reveal their route by a trail of slime, easily seen early in the day. There are several effective slug baits which are best if put down in the evening particularly in damp or showery weather. They greatly attract both pests and kill them. These baits should be placed so that they are not readily exposed to birds.

Thrips

Thrips can be troublesome on gladioli. They are tiny, black-winged insects and their larvae are minute. They hibernate on stored corms causing a grey or brown colour on the surface tissue under the scales.

This means that they will be present on the shoots when they break through the soil and that the leaves later become mottled with silvery streaks. The flowers, too, are attacked, often failing to open. The plants should be dusted with lindane as soon as the damage is seen; stored corms should be dusted with naphthalene and kept in a temperature around 10 deg. C (50°F). If affected bulbs are shaken over a piece of paper, many of these pests will fall out and can be destroyed.

Virus diseases

Virus diseases give rise to some of the most puzzling problems the gardener has to face; little is known about them and their symptoms vary greatly. Viruses are difficult to identify. They exist in the sap and reproduce at the expense of the normal proteins required by the plant. This produces a variety of symptoms such as mottling, often seen in attractive patterns, yellowing, spotting, curling, and the distortion of leaves; sometimes there are markings and blotchings on the flowers.

These diseases spread rapidly and affected plants should be burnt. The usual form of transmission is by sucking or chewing insects, notably greenfly; woodlice, thrips, eelworms and beetles are also sometimes responsible. If greenfly is seen on nearby plants all should be sprayed with derris, as these aphids commonly spread virus disorders.

It is important to wash one's hands and any implements used when destroying virus-infected plants.

Some tulips show signs of 'featherings' or 'flamings' often referred to as 'breaking'. This is caused by a virus spread by greenfly. More than one virus is responsible. Sometimes colour is added; at other times colour tones are removed. There are now some established named 'broken' tulips which are most attractive.

Sometimes bulbous plants wilt when there is no sign of disease and it is only on close examination that it becomes evident that the wilting is due to badly drained, unaerated soil or underground damage by wireworms, woodlice, etc. This calls for the application of a soil fumigant.

Yet too much must not be made of the impact of pests and disorders. If the soil is kept fed and in a healthy condition, and if sound stock is planted and maintained, diseases and pests should be kept at bay, whether in the garden, greenhouse or living room.

Allium ostrowskianum. A healthy, well-fed soil has helped to produce these superb large round umbels of pinkish flowers.

INDEX

(Figures in **bold** type refer to pictures)

ACKNOWLEDGEMENTS

The publishers wish to thank the following organizations and individuals for their kind permission to reproduce the photographs in this book.

Pat Brindley 12–13, 27, 37, 39, 43, 52 below, 66, 74–75; Robert Estall 68–69; Valerie Finnis 42; The Iris Hardwick Library 1, 61; George Hyde 77 above and below left and right; Harry Smith Horticultural Photographic Collection

6–7, 18–19, 19 below, 22, 24–25, 30–31 above, 30 below, 35, 48, 49, 60, 63; Spectrum Colour Library 14, 16 below, 21, 22–23 below, 31 below, 32, 38, 50–51, 52 above left and right, 73; Pamla Toler 56; Michael Warren 9, 20, 29, 33, 41, 44–45, 46, 47, 79. Special Photography: Melvin Grey 2–3, 4–5; Pamla Toler 16 above, 26, 28, 36, 40, 53, 54–55, 62, 67, 71. Front Cover Photograph: Pamla Toler; Back Cover Photograph: Harry Smith Horticultural Photographic Collection